easy Writer

third edition

Lex Runciman
LINFIELD COLLEGE

Carolyn Lengel

E X E R C I S E S

BEDFORD/ST. MARTIN'S
Boston ◆ New York

Manufactured in the United States of America.

0 9 8
f e d

For information, write: Bedford/St. Martin's, 75 Arlington Street, Boston, MA 02116   (617-399-4000)

ISBN-10: 0-312-44876-7
ISBN-13: 978-0-312-44876-9

EXERCISES

easy
Writer

third edition

Preface

Exercises for *EasyWriter* is a resource for teachers and students. Its exercises consist of sentences and paragraphs in need of revision; most are designed so that students can edit directly on the pages of this book.

The exercise sets are numbered to correspond to chapters in *EasyWriter,* so that students can quickly locate help by following the cross-references in each exercise's instructions.

To help students check their own progress as they work, answers to the even-numbered exercise items appear in the back of this book. Exercises with many possible answers—those asking students to imitate a sentence or revise a paragraph, for example—are not answered here. Answers to the odd-numbered exercises are given in the instructor's answer key only.

If you have adopted *EasyWriter* as a text, you are welcome to photocopy any of these exercises to use for homework assignments, classroom activities, or quizzes. The book is also available for student purchase. Also available on our Web site are additional exercises for practice: <bedfordstmartins.com/easywriter>.

Contents

SENTENCE STYLE   40

LANGUAGE   82

MULTILINGUAL WRITERS   94

ANSWERS TO THE
EVEN-NUMBERED EXERCISES   107

Find It. Fix It.

 Recognizing and eliminating the twenty most common errors

Revise each of the following numbered items to eliminate one of the twenty most common sentence-level errors written by first-year students. (See *EasyWriter*, pp. 1–10.) Example:

> it's
> **Learning another language is not a matter of genes; ~~its~~ a matter of**
> ^
> **hard work.**

1. Millie looked exhausted when she arrived from the airport. She sat her bags down in the hallway and stood there fanning her sweating face with her used plane ticket.

2. Today, we often forget how dangerous childhood diseases can be, less than a century ago, many children did not survive to adulthood because of diphtheria, whooping cough, and measles. Fortunately, such ailments are rare nowadays, however, if people decide not to immunize their children, these illnesses could easily make a comeback.

3. The Beast, which is one of the biggest roller coasters, has a thunderous ride of steep hills and turns. As you race down the first and biggest hill your coaster is engulfed by a tunnel at the end of the hill.

4. I was gaining speed and feeling really good but when I looked back he wasn't there. I panicked. I saw him and my parents down at the other end of the street and forgot to look forward. When I finally did turn forward, I saw that I was rapidly closing in on my neighbor's car.

5. I had to root for a World Series pitting the Chicago Cubs against the Boston Red Sox. Even though my brother, who believed that both teams

were historically cursed, was convinced that the world would end if either team won a pennant.

6. As teenagers, we have to make a constant effort to keep in good standing with mom and dad. After all, it is they who will support us until we are capable of living on our own with things like money, food, and clothes.

7. After deciding to begin your college career, many students are then faced with the predicament of where to live. This matter is not such a problem for students from out of town, but it is if you live in the same city or area in which you chose a school.

8. The good thing about its location is that it is right off the main highway, very easy to spot. There are also plenty of road signs pointing you in the direction of the park. And if you got extremely lost, pulling off and asking is the easiest way to get on track.

9. My children turned up their noses at anything spicy until my twelve-year-old daughters friend Georgia asked for hot sauce at our dinner table recently. I called Georgias house the next day and thanked her for convincing my kids to try something new.

10. Nancy told Lois that she needed to work overtime on Friday. This violated company rules.

11. The car broke down on the highway, and we waited hours for a tow truck to arrive. We arrived to Marisol's house almost twenty hours late, but we still made it to the ceremony.

12. Determined to find the smartest dog possible, Ed searched pet stores across the entire state. He even named his new puppy Einstein, but that didn't prevent the dog from chasing it's tail.

13. Martin Luther King Jr. Day was a holiday for years in forty-nine states, but the fiftieth, New Hampshire, did not celebrate King Day until 2000. On June 7, 1999, Governor Jeanne Shaheen of New Hampshire had finally signed into law a bill making the holiday official.

14. Is student plagiarism such a problem that professors are justified in using Web sites such as plagiarism.com to check students' work? Those university representatives who argue that students and professors should rely on an honor system believes that investigating student essays does more harm than good.

15. Drivers in parts of the country where winters are mild may need to be reminded of what to do in case the car begins to slide on a patch of ice. They should stop pressing on the accelerator avoid braking, and steer in the direction of the skid.

16. The political discussions of "family values" do not take into account the fact that divorce is not always the worst outcome for children. A child in an extremely unhappy home will not necessarily be more miserable if their parents divorce.

17. I felt someone's hand shaking my shoulder. I lifted my head up to see my best friend, Stephanie, looking down at me. "That must have been some dream. Come on the bell rang class is over."

18. In the attic, we found several old board games, that no one remembered how to play. After we found the rules for Chinese checkers on a Web site, Grandma Jo asked us to show her how to use the Internet.

19. Individual business owners rarely grant credit to customers today unless the customers sign up for a company account attached to a

credit card. Stores once use to give credit on an honor system, but most businesses no longer allow clients to run a tab.

20. The knights with armor and horses beautifully decorated participate in battles of jousting, target shooting with spears, archery, and duels of strategy and strength using swords and shields. During the evening, there is a break from the fighting, and a beautiful ceremony of marriage is acted out.

Writing

2.1 Using the Toulmin system

Use the seven-part Toulmin system to begin to develop an argument in response to one of the following questions. Here is the Toulmin system:

1. Make your claim.
2. Restate or qualify your claim.
3. Present good reasons to support your claim.
4. Explain the underlying assumptions that connect your claim and your reasons. If an underlying assumption is controversial, provide backing for it.
5. Provide additional grounds to support your claim.
6. Acknowledge and respond to possible counterarguments.
7. Draw a conclusion, stated as strongly as possible.

(See *EasyWriter*, pp. 21–22.)

1. Should the Pledge of Allegiance include the phrase "under God," or should that phrase be omitted?

2. Should schools be responsible for children's moral education, or should a child's moral development be solely the concern of the parents?

2.2 Recognizing arguable statements

Indicate which of the following sentences are arguable statements of opinion and which are factual by filling in the blank after each sentence with *arguable* or *factual*. (See *EasyWriter*, pp. 22–23.) Example:

The eradication of smallpox was the most important medical advance

of the twentieth century. <u>arguable</u>

1. Every student should learn about the ravages of smallpox. _____

2. Smallpox killed at least a third of its victims throughout recorded history. _____

3. No disease could ever be more frightening than smallpox was to people five hundred years ago. _____

4. Smallpox decimated the native populations in the Americas during the era of European exploration and colonization. _____

5. Some scholars believe that the European explorers purposefully infected native people with smallpox. _____

6. Columbus and other explorers must have realized that the people in the New World could have no immunity to European diseases. _____

7. The European interlopers and their virus destroyed cultures that were vastly superior to their own. _____

8. The World Health Organization declared in 1958 that eradicating smallpox was a worthy goal. _____

9. Smallpox, the first disease to be wiped out by human efforts, was declared dead in 1980. _____

10. The samples of smallpox virus currently kept alive in maximum-security freezers should not be destroyed because terrorist groups might also store the virus. _____

Sentence Grammar

7.1 Identifying verbs

Underline the verb in each of the following sentences. (See *Easy-Writer*, p. 58.) Example:

The governor of Illinois <u>declared</u> a moratorium on executions in his state in 2000.

1. Fourteen offenses were punishable by death in colonial America.

2. In the 1930s, most Americans still favored capital punishment.

3. However, by the late 1960s, many people in this country found capital punishment unfair and ineffective.

4. Supreme Court justices called capital punishment "cruel and unusual" when they outlawed it in 1972.

5. Most of the justices rejected the methods rather than the idea of execution itself.

6. Then, lethal injection was developed as an alternative to older execution methods such as hanging.

7. Support for capital punishment increased dramatically in the 1980s and 1990s with the rising fear of crime.

8. In the past few years, DNA evidence has given more than a hundred prisoners on death row their freedom.

9. Many Americans have said that they consider the executions of a few innocent people an acceptable price for capital punishment.

10. In 2004, the United States and China were the only industrialized nations that still used the death penalty.

7.2 Using irregular verb forms

Complete each of the following sentences by filling in each blank with the past tense or past participle of the verb listed in parentheses. (See *EasyWriter,* pp. 58–60.) Example:

Frida Kahlo ____*became*____ **(become) one of Mexico's foremost painters.**

1. Frida Kahlo _____ (grow) up in Mexico City, where she _____ (spend) most of her life.

2. She _____ (be) born in 1907, but she often _____ (say) that her birth year _____ (be) 1910.

3. In 1925 a bus accident _____ (leave) Kahlo horribly injured.

4. The accident _____ (break) her spinal column and many other bones, so Kahlo _____ (lie) in bed in a body cast for months.

5. She had always _____ (be) a spirited young woman, and she _____ (take) up painting to avoid boredom while convalescing.

6. Kahlo _____ (meet) the painter Diego Rivera in 1928 and _____ (fall) in love; they married the following year.

7. From the beginning, Rivera had _____ (know) that Kahlo's work was remarkable, so he encouraged her to paint.

8. Kahlo _____ (keep) working even though she _____ (be) in constant pain for the rest of her life.

9. Kahlo usually _____ (choose) to paint self-portraits; schol-

    ars have _____ (begin) to analyze her unflinching vision of

    herself.

10. The fame of Frida Kahlo has _____ (grow) and

    _____ (spread) since her death in 1954.

7.3 Editing verb forms

Where necessary, edit the following sentences to eliminate any inappropriate verb forms. If the verb forms in a sentence are correct
as printed, write C. (See *EasyWriter,* pp. 58 – 60.) Example:

> began
> She ~~begin~~ the examination on time.
>   ^

1. The tickets costed almost a hundred dollars apiece, so we decided

    not to see the concert.

2. The lake freezed early this year.

3. The band had sang its last song before the fight begun.

4. Please don't make us any dinner; we have already ate.

5. They had felt that tired only once before.

6. Everyone was shaken up by the turbulence, but the plane landed

    safely.

7. We brung baked beans to the potluck dinner.

8. The accountants must have knowed what the CEO was up to when

    he looted the company.

9. By the mid-1970s, New York had almost went bankrupt.

10. Over the years, Martin has become a close friend.

7.4 Distinguishing between *lie* and *lay*, *sit* and *set*, *rise* and *raise*

Choose the appropriate verb form in each of the following sentences. (See *EasyWriter,* pp. 60–61.) Example:

The boys laid/<u>lay</u> on the couch, hoping for something good on TV.

1. I sat/set back, closed my eyes, and began to meditate.

2. Mrs. Worth struggled to rise/raise herself to her feet when the judge entered the courtroom.

3. In this area, when the temperature rises/raises, the humidity usually declines.

4. The choir rose/raised up and belted out a hymn.

5. Sitting/Setting in the sun too long can lead to skin cancer.

6. The students sat/set their backpacks down beside their desks and stared grimly at the new teacher.

7. He used whatever was lying/laying around the house.

8. As the flag rose/raised, a trumpeter played "Taps."

9. I lay/laid my books down just as the telephone rang.

10. Sometimes she just lies/lays and stares at the ceiling.

7.5 Deciding on verb tenses

Complete each of the following sentences by filling in the blank with an appropriate form of the verb given in parentheses. Because more than one form will sometimes be possible, choose one form and then be prepared to explain the reasons for your choice. (See *EasyWriter,* pp. 61–62.) Example:

Many people __*come/came/have come*__ (come) to the United States

seeking religious freedom.

The present tense *come* is appropriate if the sentence states a general truth about immigration; the past tense *came* is appropriate if the sentence refers to immigration at a specific time in the past; the present perfect tense *have come* is appropriate if the sentence refers to immigration that either continues today or ended at an unspecified time in the past. Because the sentence does not provide any information about the time frame to which it refers, any of these answers is acceptable.

1. Every American schoolchild _____ (learn) about the first Thanksgiving.

2. It is true that the Puritans _____ (invite) the most important members of the Wampanoag tribe to join them for the three-day feast.

3. Massasoit and his people _____ (help) the Puritan colony survive during the bitter winter of 1620–1621, so the Puritans thanked them with a harvest celebration.

4. The harvest feast _____ (be) not typical of relations among Puritan colonists and northeastern tribes.

5. Scholars today _____ (conclude) that the Wampanoags and the colonists _____ (disagree) about land use, religion, and other important issues.

6. In an attempt to control the tribes, the colonists _____ (interrogate) Wamsutta, Massasoit's son and successor, in 1662; he _____ (die) shortly afterward.

7. Wamsutta's brother Metacom, known as King Philip, _____ (attack) the colonists in 1675, leading to more than a year of the worst bloodshed the colonies _____ (see).

8. Before the late nineteenth century, most representations of Puritans and Native Americans _____ (show) violent confrontations.

9. While the Indian wars _____ (happen) in the West, images of European colonists and native tribes coexisting peacefully were not popular in the United States.

10. The idea of the peaceful dinner _____ (begin) to appeal to Americans in the twentieth century, when cooperation among different ethnic groups _____ (become) a priority.

7.6   Sequencing tenses

Change the italicized word or phrase in each of the following sentences to create the appropriate sequence of tenses. If a sentence reads acceptably, write C. (See *EasyWriter*, p. 63.) Example:

>   *have sent*
> **He needs *to ~~send~~* in his application before today.**

1. The crew *had dug* the trench before they installed the cable.

2. Until I started knitting again last month, I *have forgotten* how.

3. *Having sung* in the shower, he did not hear the doorbell.

4. After Darius said that he wanted to postpone college, I *am trying* to talk him out of it.

5. Will you tell Grandpa about your wedding plans when he *has visited* us in the summer?

6. They *hoped* to plant their garden by now.

7. You *will have finished* your paper by the time the semester ends.

8. When he was twenty-one, he *wanted to become* a millionaire by the age of thirty.

9. The news had just begun when our power *goes* out.

10. *Cutting off* all contact with family, he had no one to ask for help.

7.7 Converting the voice of a sentence

Convert each sentence from active to passive voice or from passive to active, and note the differences in emphasis these changes make. (See *EasyWriter*, p. 63.) Example:

Machiavelli advises the prince to gain the friendship of the people.

The prince is advised by Machiavelli to gain the friendship of the people.

1. The blog "Talking Points Memo" is maintained by Joshua Micah Marshall.

2. Huge pine trees were uprooted by the storm.

3. Have any spiders been seen in the basement lately?

4. The last doughnut in the box was eaten by Jerry just a few minutes ago.

5. The experimental data are analyzed in the next section of this report.

6. For months, the baby kangaroo is protected, fed, and taught how to survive by its mother.

7. An American teenager narrates DBC Pierre's prizewinning novel about a Columbine-like school shooting, *Vernon God Little*.

8. The lawns and rooftops were covered with the first snow of winter.

9. Marianne avoided such things as elevators, subways, and closets.

10. Suddenly, rainfall pounded on the roof over our heads.

7.8 Using the subjunctive mood

Revise any of the following sentences that do not use the appropriate subjunctive verb forms required in formal or academic writing. If the verb forms in a sentence are appropriate as printed, write C. (See *EasyWriter*, pp. 63–65.) Example:

were
He moved carefully, as if he ~~was~~ caring for an infant.
‸

1. Even if I was rich, I wouldn't buy those overpriced shoes.

2. The family requested that contributions be made in Gertrude's memory to a Democratic presidential candidate.

3. The lawyer made it seem as if I was a threat to society.

4. Marie would have gone to the Patti Smith show on New Year's Eve if she would have heard about it in advance.

5. I wish I was with you right now.

6. It is necessary that the manager knows how to do any job in the store.

7. Her stepsisters treated Cinderella as though she was a servant.

8. The invisible announcer requested that audience members should not take photographs.

9. The only requirement is that the tense of both clauses makes sense.

10. If more money was available, we would be able to offer more student scholarships.

8.1 Selecting verbs that agree with their subjects

Underline the appropriate verb form in each of the following sentences. (See *EasyWriter*, pp. 65–70.) Example:

Experts on every subject is / <u>are</u> easy to find on the Internet.

1. The desire to find information and answers sends/send many people on Internet searches.

2. There is/are many people eager to offer advice online.

3. What credentials does/do these so-called experts have?

4. Problems with using the Internet includes/include the difficulty of determining which sources are reliable.

5. Everyone with access to a computer and a modem has/have the ability to send information over the Internet.

6. Some people put up Web pages that offers/offer impressive but inaccurate data.

7. If a delusional science fiction buff and a respected professor of cosmology writes/write about a new comet, the latter will probably provide better research.

8. To some people, everything on the Internet looks/look equally convincing.

9. A slick design and an eye-catching graphic does/do not mean that the information provided on a Web page is accurate.

10. Learning how to navigate the Web and conduct searches does/do not take the place of developing critical thinking skills.

8.2 Making subjects and verbs agree

Revise the following sentences as necessary to establish subject-verb agreement. If a sentence does not require any change, write *C*. (See *EasyWriter*, pp. 65–70.) Example:

                                            has

A new museum displaying O. Winston Link's photographs ~~have~~

                                            ^

opened in Roanoke, Virginia.

1. Anyone interested in steam locomotives have probably already heard of the photographer O. Winston Link.

2. Imagine that it are the 1950s, and Link is creating his famous photographs.

3. The steam locomotives—the "iron horses" of the nineteenth century— has begun to give way to diesel engines.

4. Only the Norfolk & Western rail line's Appalachian route still use steam engines.

5. Link, a specialist in public relations, is also a commercial photographer and train lover.

6. He and his assistant Thomas Garver sets up nighttime shots of steam locomotives.

7. Days of setup is required for a single flash photo of a train passing by.

8. Many of the photos show scenes that would have been totally in the dark without Link's flashbulbs.

9. Up to sixteen flashbulbs and specialized reflectors illuminates every important detail.

10. Link's fine photographic eye and his ability to imagine how the flash will look allows him to compose each photo in advance in the dark.

11. His book *Steam, Steel, and Stars* include most of his stunning nighttime train photographs.

12. Famous Link photos such as one of a steam engine passing a drive-in movie appear in the book.

13. Today, the photographs of O. Winston Link has a cult following.

14. More than two thousand negatives from the steam locomotive era belongs to the O. Winston Link Museum in Roanoke.

15. Almost everyone who has seen a Link photograph remembers it.

9.1 Identifying adjectives and adverbs

Identify the adjectives and adverbs in each of the following sentences, underlining the adjectives once and the adverbs twice. Remember that articles and some pronouns can function as adjectives. (See *EasyWriter*, pp. 71–72.) Example:

> <u>Uncomfortable</u> in <u>his</u> <u>increasingly</u> <u>tight</u> jeans, he rejected <u>a</u> <u>second</u>
>
> dessert.

1. Politicians must seriously consider how well their lives will withstand intense public scrutiny.

2. Time passed agonizingly slowly, but midnight finally arrived.

3. The shoes in that store are lovely, uncomfortably narrow, and much too expensive.

4. The somewhat shy author spoke reluctantly to six exuberant admirers.

5. I do not want any more of your sorry excuses.

6. The youngest dancer in the troupe performed a brilliant solo.

7. The most instructive of the books is, unfortunately, the longest.

8. Never before has one politician made a bigger mess in this amount of time.

9. Late in the day, the temperature dropped precipitously.

10. Imminent starvation threatens many populations constantly.

9.2 Adding adjectives and adverbs

Expand each of the following sentences by adding appropriate adjectives and adverbs. Delete *the* if need be. (See *EasyWriter*, pp. 71–72.) Example:

> Then three   thoroughly   nervous
> ⊼he veterinarians examined the patient.
>   ^   ^   ^   ^

1. Our assignment is due Wednesday.

2. Most of us enjoy movies.

3. Her superiors praised her work for the Environmental Protection Agency.

4. A corporation can fire workers.

5. The heroine marries the prince.

6. The boardwalk crosses the beach.

7. I have neglected my friend.

8. The media are ignoring his candidacy.

9. Nobody saw the bear, but the ranger said it was dangerous.

10. Which way did you say the pair went?

9.3 Using adjectives and adverbs appropriately

Revise each of the following sentences to correct adverb and adjective use. Then, for each adjective and adverb you've revised, point out the word that it modifies. (See *EasyWriter*, pp. 71–72.) Example:

commonly

Almost every language ~~common~~ uses nonverbal cues that people can interpret.

1. Most people understand easy that raised eyebrows indicate surprise.

2. When a man defiant crosses his arms across his chest, you probably do not need to ask what the gesture means.

3. You are sure familiar with the idea that bodily motions are a kind of language, but is the same thing true of nonverbal sounds?

4. If you feel sadly, your friends may express sympathy by saying, "Awww."

5. When food tastes well, diners express their satisfaction by murmuring, "Mmmm!"

6. If you feel relievedly that a long day is finally over, you may say, "Whew!"

7. These nonverbal signals are called "paralanguage," and they are quick becoming an important field of linguistic study.

8. Paralanguage "words" may look oddly on paper.

9. Written words can only partial indicate what paralanguage sounds like.

10. Lucky for linguists today, tape recorders are readily available.

9.4 Using comparative and superlative modifiers appropriately

Revise each of the following sentences to use modifiers correctly, clearly, and effectively. A variety of acceptable answers is possible for each sentence. (See *EasyWriter,* pp. 72–73.) Example:

> **When Macbeth and Lady Macbeth plot to kill the king, she shows**
> more
> **herself to be the ~~most~~ ambitious of the two.**
> ^

1. The Van Gogh painting was the most priceless.

2. Most of the elderly are women because women tend to live longer.

3. My graduation day will be the most happiest day of my life.

4. Minneapolis is the largest of the Twin Cities.

5. Many couples preparing to marry now arrange for a longer engagement.

6. St. Francis made Assisi one of the famousest towns in Italy.

7. Our team sampled Jujubes, Goldberg's Peanut Chews, and Milk Duds to see which candy was easier on our teeth.

8. That trip to the dentist for a root canal was the unpleasantest experience of my life.

9. You could have found a more nicer way to thank your grandmother for the gift.

10. She has the most unique laugh.

10.1 Revising sentences with misplaced modifiers

Revise each of the following sentences by moving any misplaced modifiers so that they clearly modify the words they are intended to. You may have to change grammatical structures for some sentences. (See *EasyWriter*, p. 74.) Example:

> **Elderly people and students live in the neighborhood**
> full of identical tract houses
> **surrounding the university/.which is full of identical tract houses.**

1. Doctors recommend a new test for cancer, which is painless.

2. The tenor captivated the entire audience singing with verve.

3. I went through the process of taxiing and taking off in my mind.

4. The city approximately spent twelve million dollars on the new stadium.

5. Am I the only person who cares about modifiers in sentences that are misplaced?

6. On the day in question, the patient was not normally able to breathe.

7. Refusing to die at the end of the play, the audience stared in amazement at the actor playing Hamlet.

8. The clothes were full of holes that I was giving away.

9. Revolving out of control, the maintenance worker shut down the turbine.

10. A wailing baby was quickly kissed by the candidate with a soggy diaper.

10.2 Revising squinting modifiers, disruptive modifiers, and split infinitives

Revise each of the following sentences by moving disruptive modifiers and split infinitives as well as by repositioning any squinting modifier so that it unambiguously modifies either the word(s) before it or the word(s) after it. You may have to add words to a sentence to revise it adequately. (See *EasyWriter*, pp. 74–75.) Example:

The course we hoped would engross us completely bored us.

The course we hoped would completely engross us bored us.
OR
The course we hoped would engross us bored us completely.

1. Airline security personnel asked Ishmael, while he was hurrying to make his connecting flight, to remove his shoes and socks and to open his carry-on bag.

2. He remembered vividly enjoying the sound of Mrs. McIntosh's singing.

3. Bookstores sold, in the first week after publication, fifty thousand copies.

4. The mayor promised after her reelection she would not raise taxes.

5. The exhibit, because of extensive publicity, attracted large audiences.

6. The collector who owned the painting originally planned to leave it to a museum.

7. Doug hoped to this time succeed in training the cat to stay in one place even when it was not sleeping.

8. Doctors can now restore limbs that have been severed partially to a functioning condition.

9. A new housing development has gone up with six enormous homes on the hill across the road from Mr. Jacoby's farm.

10. The speaker said when he finished he would answer questions.

11. People who swim frequently will improve their physical condition.

12. The compost smelled after a long summer under the blazing sun pretty bad when I turned it.

13. The state commission promised at its final meeting to make its recommendations public.

14. Stella did not want to argue, after a long day at work and an evening class, about who was going to do the dishes.

15. In the next several months, Lynn hopes to despite her busy schedule of entertaining maintain her diet and actually lose weight.

10.3　Revising dangling modifiers

Revise each of the following sentences to correct the dangling modifiers. (See *EasyWriter*, pp. 75–76.) Example:

> *a viewer gets*
> **Watching television news, an impression ~~is given~~ of constant disaster.**
> ⌃

1. High ratings are pursued by emphasizing fires and murders.

2. Interviewing grieving relatives, no consideration is shown for their privacy.

3. To provide comic relief, heat waves and blizzards are attributed to the weather forecaster.

4. Chosen for their looks, the newscasters' journalistic credentials are often weak.

5. As a visual medium, complex issues are hard to present in a televised format.

6. Assumed to care about no one except Americans, editorial boards for network news shows reject many international stories.

7. Generally only twenty-two minutes long, not including commercials, viewers have little time to absorb information.

8. Horrified by stories of bloodshed, the low probability of becoming a victim of crime or terrorism goes unrecognized.

9. Increasing fears among viewers, Americans worry about unlikely events such as children being kidnapped by strangers.

10. Not covering less sensational but more common dangers such as reckless driving and diabetes, viewers may not understand what is really likely to hurt them.

11. Long respected as the best source of news, many readers do not notice their newspapers' flaws and biases.

12. Reporting on a national story, many articles focus on speculation about causes instead of on what actually happened.

13. Influenced subtly by reporters' opinions, newspapers may actually change perceptions of truth.

14. Whether listening to talk radio or watching political talk shows on television, distortions and bias are the norm.

15. By not getting the facts needed to make informed decisions, the news media could do a better job.

11.1 Identifying pronouns and antecedents

Identify the pronouns and any antecedents in each of the following sentences, underlining the pronouns once and any antecedents twice. (See *EasyWriter,* pp. 76–81.) Example:

A guide <u>dog</u> must handle <u>itself</u> well in any situation.

1. Everyone has seen a guide dog at some time in his or her life.

2. Guide dogs that work with the blind must act as their human partners' eyes.

3. These dogs learn socialization and basic obedience training when they are puppies.

4. Knowing they will have to give up their dog one day, sighted volunteers agree to live with and train a puppy for the first year of its life.

5. Puppies that are destined to be guide dogs are allowed to go into places that routinely refuse entry to other kinds of dogs.

6. If you see a puppy in a supermarket or an office, look for its special coat that identifies it as a trainee guide dog.

7. Volunteer trainers miss their pups after the training period ends, but nothing is more rewarding than knowing that the pups will make life easier for their new owners.

8. Some of the pups do not pass the requirements to become guide dogs, but these are in great demand as household pets.

9. When a dog passes the test and graduates, it and its blind companion learn to work with each other during an intensive training session.

10. If you are interested in learning about guide dogs or in becoming a volunteer, contact your local school for the blind.

11.2 Using subjective-case pronouns

Replace the underlined noun or nouns in each of the following sentences with the appropriate subjective case pronoun. (See *EasyWriter*, pp. 76–79.) Example:

he
Jack and ~~George~~ visited the new science library.
^

1. The person who got the highest mark on the test was <u>Susan</u>.

2. Whenever <u>Jerry, David, and Sean</u> went to the beach, the weather was bad.

3. As the sun rose that morning, Melina considered how lucky <u>Melina</u> was to be able to see it.

4. As the cattle crossed the road, <u>the cattle</u> stopped all traffic.

5. Justin, Paolo, and I have a great time whenever <u>Justin, Paolo, and I</u> get together.

6. The library has a collection of Mark Twain's manuscripts, but <u>the manuscripts</u> are not available to the general public.

7. The cars slowed to a stop whenever <u>the cars</u> approached an on-ramp.

8. <u>Tina, Rahul, Fredo, and I</u> stayed up all night watching the complete box set of *The Godfather* on DVD.

9. Fredo decided that <u>Fredo</u> did not like the scene where Michael has his own brother killed.

10. Maya wondered if <u>Maya</u> were smarter than James.

11.3 Using objective-case pronouns

Most of the following sentences use pronouns incorrectly. Revise the incorrect sentences so that they contain correct objective-case pronouns. If a sentence is correct, write C. (See *EasyWriter*, pp. 76–79.) Example:

> me
> **Eventually, the headwaiter told Kim, Stanley, and I̶ that we could be seated.**

1. Which of the twins are you waiting for — Mary or he?

2. The president gave her the highest praise.

3. Which of those books is for myself?

4. When we asked, the seller promised we that the software would work on a Macintosh computer.

5. Though even the idea of hang gliding made herself nervous, she gave it a try.

6. Max told Jackson and him that the cabin was available to they.

7. Cycling thirty miles a day was triathlon training for Bill, Ubijo, and I.

8. Dennis asked her and me to speak to him in the office.

9. Between you and I, that essay doesn't deserve a high grade.

10. We need two volunteers: yourself and Tom.

11.4 Using possessive-case pronouns

Insert a possessive pronoun in the blank in each sentence. (See *EasyWriter*, pp. 76–79.) Example:

> ____My____ **girlfriend bought flowers for me on Valentine's Day.**

1. All day long, people in the office asked admiringly, "_____ flowers are those?"

2. I told them the bouquet was _____ .

3. The arrangement was perfectly complemented by _____ vase, which my girlfriend had chosen.

4. _____ selection for me was red roses.

5. Every flower has _____ own meaning, according to a Victorian tradition.

6. Roses are easy to understand; _____ meaning is "true love."

7. My girlfriend knows that roses are my favorite flower; _____ are daffodils.

8. I really appreciated _____ going to the trouble and expense of buying me flowers.

9. Not only was it Valentine's Day, but she and I were also celebrating the anniversary of _____ first date.

10. That's the story of my most romantic moment; now tell me _____ .

11.5 Using *who, whoever, whom,* or *whomever*

Insert *who, whoever, whom,* or *whomever* appropriately in the blank in each of the following sentences. (See *EasyWriter,* pp. 77–78.) Example:

She is someone ____who____ will go far.

1. Professor Quinones asked _____ we wanted to collaborate with.

2. _____ the director chooses to play the lead roles will have to put up with the writer's tantrums.

3. _____ shall I say is calling?

4. Soap operas appeal to _____ is interested in intrigue, suspense, joy, pain, grief, romance, fidelity, sex, and violence.

5. The manager promised to reward _____ sold the most cars.

6. _____ will the new tax law benefit most?

7. The plumbers _____ the landlord hired to install the new toilets in the building have botched the job.

8. The only experts _____ they can recommend are the two magicians who trained them.

9. _____ the voters choose faces an almost impossible challenge.

10. The ballroom is available for children's parties or for _____ wants to rent it.

11.6 **Using pronouns in compound structures, appositives, elliptical clauses; choosing between *we* and *us* before a noun**

Choose the appropriate pronoun from the pair in parentheses in each of the following sentences. (See *EasyWriter,* pp. 78–79.) Example:

Of the group, only (she/her) and I finished the race.

1. All the other job applicants were far more experienced than (I/me).

2. Only (he/him) and the two dressmakers knew what his top-secret fall line would be like.

3. When Jessica and (she/her) first met, they despised each other.

4. Samantha sighed, "I love Benicio del Toro. No one could ever be more beautiful than (he/him)."

5. To (we/us) New Englanders, hurricanes are a bigger worry than tornadoes.

6. The post-holiday credit card bills were a rude shock to Gary and (she/her).

7. Tomorrow (we/us) raw recruits will have our first on-the-job test.

8. The relationship between (they/them) and their brother was often strained.

9. You may think that Anita will win Miss Congeniality, but in fact, everyone likes you better than (she/her).

10. Keith Richards scoffed at the words "Sir Mick Jagger," but (he/him) and Mick apparently don't agree about knighthood.

11. Just between you and (I/me), this seminar is a disaster!

12. Staying a week in a lakeside cabin gave (we/us) New Yorkers a much-needed vacation.

13. Lute Johannson always claimed he was the best of (we/us) chili cookers.

14. Jason is younger than (I/me).

15. Seeing (he and I/him and me) dressed up in her best clothes made Mom laugh until she saw the lipstick on the rug.

11.7 Maintaining pronoun–antecedent agreement

Revise the following sentences as needed to create pronoun-antecedent agreement and to eliminate the generic *he* and any awkward pronoun references. Some sentences can be revised in more than one way, and two sentences do not require any change. If a sentence is correct as written, write *C*. (See *EasyWriter*, pp. 79–80.) Example:

Everyone should make his own decision about having children.

Everyone should make his or her own decision about having children.
OR
All individuals should make their own decision about having children.

1. Someone who chooses not to have any children of his own is often known today as "child-free" rather than "childless."

2. A child-free person may feel that people with children see his time as less valuable than their own.

3. Corporate culture sometimes offers parents more time off and other perks than it provides to non-parents.

4. A child-free employee may feel that they have to subsidize family medical plans at work for people who have children.

5. Neither parents nor a child-free person has the right to insist that their childbearing choice is the only correct one to make.

6. However, a community has to consider the welfare of their children because caring for and educating children eventually benefits everyone.

7. Neither an educated citizenry nor a skilled workforce can exist if they are not financed and helped by older generations.

8. Almost no one would be able to afford to have children if they were expected to pay for educating and training their offspring entirely without help.

9. People who feel that they should not have to help pay for quality day care and schools have not thought through their responsibilities and needs as members of society.

10. As writer Barbara Kingsolver once pointed out, even someone without children will probably need the services of a doctor or a mechanic in their old age.

11.8 Clarifying pronoun reference

Revise each of the following sentences to clarify pronoun reference. All the items can be revised in more than one way. If a pronoun refers ambiguously to more than one possible antecedent, revise the sentence to reflect each possible meaning. (See *EasyWriter*, pp. 80–81.) Example:

After Jane left, Miranda found her keys.

Miranda found Jane's keys after Jane left.

Miranda found her own keys after Jane left.

1. Quint trusted Smith because she had worked for her before.

2. Not long after the company set up the subsidiary, it went bankrupt.

3. When drug therapy is combined with psychotherapy, patients relate better to their therapists, are less vulnerable to what disturbs them, and are more responsive to them.

4. When Deyon was reunited with his father, he wept.

5. Bill smilingly announced his promotion to Ed.

6. On the weather forecast, it said to expect snow in the overnight hours.

7. The tragedy of child abuse is that even after the children of abusive parents grow up, they often continue the sad tradition of cruelty.

8. Lear divides his kingdom between the two older daughters, Goneril and Regan, whose extravagant professions of love are more flattering than the simple affection of the youngest daughter, Cordelia. The consequences of this error in judgment soon become apparent, as they prove neither grateful nor kind to him.

9. Anna smiled at her mother as she opened the birthday gift.

10. The visit to the pyramids was canceled because of recent terrorist attacks on tourists there, which disappointed Kay, who had waited years to see them.

11.9 Revising to clarify pronoun reference

Revise the following paragraph to establish a clear antecedent for every pronoun that needs one. (See *EasyWriter,* pp. 80–81.)

In Paul Fussell's essay "My War," he writes about his experience in combat during World War II, which he says still haunts his life. Fussell confesses that he joined the infantry ROTC in 1939 as a way of getting out of gym class, where he would have been forced to expose his "fat and flabby" body to the ridicule of his classmates. However, it proved to be a serious miscalculation. After the United States entered the war in 1941, other male college students were able to join officer training programs in specialized fields that kept them out of combat. If you were already in an ROTC unit associated with the infantry, though, you were trapped in it. That was how Fussell came to be shipped to France as a rifle-platoon leader in 1944. Almost immediately they sent him to the front, where he soon developed pneumonia because of insufficient winter clothing. He spent a month in hospitals; because he did not want to worry his parents, however, he told them it was just the flu. When he returned to the front, he was wounded by a shell that killed his sergeant.

12.1 Revising comma splices and fused sentences

Revise each of the following comma splices or fused sentences by using the method suggested in brackets after the sentence. (See *EasyWriter,* pp. 82–84.) Example:

but
Americans think of slavery as a problem of the past, it still exists
                                              ^
in some parts of the world. [Join with a comma and a coordinating
conjunction.]

1. We tend to think of slavery only in U.S. terms in fact, it began long
    before the United States existed and still goes on. [Separate into two
    sentences.]

2. The group Human Rights Watch filed a report on Mauritania, it is a
    nation in northwest Africa. [Recast as one independent clause.]

3. Slavery has existed in Mauritania for centuries it continues today.
    [Join with a comma and a coordinating conjunction.]

4. Members of Mauritania's ruling group are called the Beydanes, they are
    an Arab Berber tribe also known as the White Moors. [Recast as one
    independent clause.]

5. Another group in Mauritania is known as the Haratin or the Black
    Moors, they are native West Africans. [Separate into two sentences.]

6. In modern-day Mauritania many of the Haratin are still slaves, they
    serve the Beydanes. [Join with a semicolon.]

7. The first modern outcry against slavery in Mauritania arose in 1980,
    protesters objected to the public sale of an enslaved woman. [Recast as
    an independent and a dependent clause.]

8. Mauritania outlawed slavery in 1981 little has been done to enforce the
    law. [Join with a comma and a coordinating conjunction.]

9. The law promised slaveholders financial compensation for freeing their
    slaves however, the language of the law did not explain exactly who
    would come up with the money. [Join with a semicolon.]

10. Physical force is not usually used to enslave the Haratin, rather, they are held by the force of conditioning. [Separate into two sentences.]

11. In some ways the Mauritanian system is different from slavery in the United States, there are few slave rebellions in Mauritania. [Join with a comma and a coordinating conjunction.]

12. By some estimates 300,000 former slaves still serve their old masters these slaves are psychologically and economically dependent. [Recast as an independent and a dependent clause.]

13. Many Mauritanian slaves live in their own houses, they may work for their former masters in exchange for a home or for food or medical care. [Recast as an independent and a dependent clause.]

14. In addition, there may be as many as 90,000 Haratin still enslaved, some Beydanes have refused to free their slaves unless the government pays compensation. [Join with a semicolon.]

15. Some Mauritanians claim that slavery is not a problem in their country in fact, in 2001, a Mauritanian official told a United Nations committee that slavery had never existed there. [Join with a dash.]

16. Of course, slavery must have existed in Mauritania there would have been no compelling reason to make a decree to abolish it in 1981. [Join with a comma and a coordinating conjunction.]

17. The president of Mauritania insisted in 1997 that discussions of modern slavery were intended only to hurt the country's reputation his comments did not offer much hope for opponents of slavery. [Recast as an independent and a dependent clause.]

18. Both the slaveholding Beydanes and the enslaved Haratin are made up largely of Muslims, some people in Mauritania see resistance to slavery

in their country as anti-Muslim. [Join with a comma and a coordinating conjunction.]

19. In some cases, Western opponents of Mauritanian slavery may indeed harbor anti-Muslim sentiments that fact does not justify allowing the slavery to continue. [Join with a semicolon.]

20. Islamic authorities in Mauritania have agreed that all Muslims are equal therefore, one Muslim must not enslave another. [Join with a semicolon.]

12.2 Revising comma splices

Revise the following paragraph, eliminating all comma splices by using a period or a semicolon. Then revise the paragraph again, this time using any of these three methods:

Separate independent clauses into sentences of their own.

Recast two or more clauses as one independent clause.

Recast one independent clause as a dependent clause.

Comment on the two revisions. What differences in rhythm do you detect? Which version do you prefer, and why? (See *EasyWriter*, pp. 82–84.)

My sister Mary decided to paint her house last spring, thus, she had to buy some paint. She wanted inexpensive paint, at the same time, it had to go on easily and cover well, that combination was unrealistic to start with. She had never done exterior painting before, in fact, she did not even own a ladder. She was a complete beginner, on the other hand, she was a hard worker and was willing to learn. She got her husband, Dan, to take a week off from work, likewise she let her two teenage sons take three days off from school to help. Mary went out and bought dark green paint for $6.99 a gallon, it must have been mostly water, in fact, you could almost see through it. Mary and Dan and the boys put one coat of this paint on the house, as a result, their white house turned a streaky light green. Dan and the boys rebelled, declaring they would not work anymore with such cheap paint. Mary was forced to buy all new paint, even so, the house did not really get painted until September.

12.3 Revising comma splices and fused sentences

Revise the following paragraph, eliminating the comma splices and fused sentences by using any of these methods:

Separate independent clauses into sentences of their own.

Link clauses with a comma and a coordinating conjunction.

Link clauses with a semicolon and, perhaps, a conjunctive adverb or a transitional phrase.

Recast two or more clauses as one independent clause.

Recast one independent clause as a dependent clause.

Link clauses with a dash.

Then revise the paragraph again, this time eliminating each comma splice and fused sentence by using a different method. Decide which paragraph is more effective, and why. Finally, compare the revision you prefer with the revisions of several other students, and discuss the ways in which the versions differ in meaning. (See *EasyWriter*, pp. 82–84.)

When most Americans think of drug dealers, they picture a shadowy figure in a dark alley, there are illicit drug deals in small-town homes and farmhouses, too. A recent survey of young Americans provided evidence that rural teens are more likely than urban ones to use illegal drugs, the young people's drugs of choice include not only marijuana but also methamphetamine and other substances. Meth labs seem to be appearing in more and more small towns these chemical labs are easy and inexpensive to set up in a home or an outbuilding. Methamphetamine addiction is on the rise in rural America, a fact that is devastating to local communities and shocking to those who live elsewhere. Outsiders are likely to forget that rural

America is frequently impoverished the teens in poor rural areas are as likely as urban youth to feel bored and trapped in a dead-end existence. Open country and trees are all very well, if there are no jobs, can young people live on bucolic scenery? Many of these teens have seen their parents struggle they cannot really expect their lives to be significantly different. A rural upbringing can't protect children from drugs ensuring that they have hope and constructive ways to spend their time is a much more effective deterrent.

13.1 Eliminating sentence fragments

Revise each of the following fragments, either by combining fragments with independent clauses or by rewriting them as separate sentences. (See *EasyWriter,* pp. 84–86.) Example:

> **Zoe looked close to tears. Standing with her head bowed.**
>
> Standing with her head bowed, Zoe looked close to tears.
>
> Zoe looked close to tears. She was standing with her head bowed.

1. Wollstonecraft believed in universal public education. Also, in education that forms the heart and strengthens the body.

2. Her father pulled strings to get her the job. Later regretting his actions.

3. Organized crime has been able to attract graduates just as big business has. With good pay and the best equipment money can buy.

4. Trying to carry a portfolio, art box, illustration boards, and drawing pads. I must have looked ridiculous.

5. The president promoted one tax change. A reduction in the capital gains tax.

6. Connie picked up the cat and started playing with it. It scratched her neck. With its sharp little claws.

7. The climbers had two choices. To go over a four-hundred-foot cliff or to turn back. They decided to make the attempt.

8. The region has dry, sandy soil. Blown into strange formations by the ever-present wind.

9. The appeal of this film is obvious. Its enthusiastic embrace of sex and violence.

10. To feel useful. Many older Americans want nothing more than that.

13.2 Revising a paragraph to eliminate sentence fragments

Underline every fragment you find in the following paragraph. Then revise the paragraph. You may combine or rearrange sentences as long as you retain the original content. (See *EasyWriter,* pp. 84–86.)

It must be embarrassing for famous people. To have people think that they are dead when they aren't. I'm not talking about whispered conspiracies. Like all of those supposed clues on Beatles albums about Paul McCartney's supposed demise. (In case you were wondering. Paul is alive and well and now a knight, no less.) Instead, I'm thinking about half-forgotten celebrities. Actors and musicians who are not among your favorites may get mixed up in your mind. Before you know it. You're saying to a friend, "I thought that guy was dead." Then you may both debate for a while. Because neither of you is certain whether the guy really is dead or whether you're thinking of someone else who sort of resembled him. It's a good thing so many celebrity reality shows and exposés feature the has-beens you barely remember. With those shows. You at least know that the people on screen are still alive. Or if they aren't. They have died recently enough that you will probably still remember.

13.3 Understanding intentional fragments

Choose an advertisement from a newspaper or magazine that contains intentional fragments. Rewrite the advertisement to eliminate all sentence fragments. Be prepared to explain how your version and the original differ in impact and why you think the copywriters for the ad chose to use fragments rather than complete sentences. (See *EasyWriter,* pp. 84–86.)

Sentence Style

14.1 Matching subjects and predicates

Revise each of the following sentences in two ways to make its structures consistent in grammar and meaning. (See *EasyWriter*, p. 89.) Example:

> **By studying African American folklore and biblical stories have influenced Toni Morrison's fiction.**
>
> African American folklore and biblical stories have influenced Toni Morrison's fiction.
>
> Toni Morrison's study of African American folklore and biblical stories has influenced her fiction.

1. Toni Morrison's grandmother, who moved to Ohio from the South with only fifteen dollars to her name, and Morrison had great respect for her.

2. In her books, many of which deal with the aftermath of slavery, often feature strong women characters.

3. Published in 1970, Morrison's first novel, *The Bluest Eye*, the story of a young African American girl who wants to look like her Shirley Temple doll.

4. Although Morrison's depictions of African American families and neighborhoods are realistic, but they also include supernatural elements.

5. An important character in Morrison's 1977 novel *Song of Solomon* is about Pilate, a woman with magical powers.

6. *Song of Solomon*, hailed as a masterpiece, winning the National Book Critics Circle Award in 1978.

7. Morrison's fame as a writer won the Pulitzer Prize in fiction in 1988 for *Beloved*.

8. The title character in *Beloved* features the ghost of a murdered infant inhabiting the body of a young woman.

9. When reading *Beloved* makes the horrors of American slavery seem immediate and real.

10. In 1993, Toni Morrison, who became the first African American woman to be awarded the Nobel Prize in literature.

14.2 Making comparisons complete, consistent, and clear

Revise each of the following sentences to eliminate any inappropriate elliptical constructions; to make comparisons complete, logically consistent, and clear; and to supply any other omitted words that are necessary for meaning. (See *EasyWriter*, p. 90.) Example:

                                      is
Most of the candidates are bright, and one brilliant.

1. Tim decided to take a nap, Michael decided to study for his chemistry test, and Susan to take a book back to the library.

2. New York City has a more diverse culture than any metropolis in the United States.

3. Laws governing drug use in Canada are more liberal than the United States.

4. As time went on, the baby became less animated and interested.

5. Argentina and Peru were colonized by Spain, and Brazil by Portugal.

6. The car's exterior is blue, but the seats black vinyl.

7. The house is Victorian, its windows enormous.

8. Are citizens of the United States now as safe or safer than they were before September 11, 2001?

9. My new stepmother makes my father happier.

10. She argued that children are even more important for men than women.

14.3 Revising for consistency and completeness

Revise this passage so that all sentences are grammatically and logically consistent and complete. (See *EasyWriter*, pp. 88–90.)

A concentrated animal feeding operation, or CAFO, is when a factory farm raises thousands of animals in a confined space. Vast amounts of factory-farm livestock waste, dumped into giant lagoons, which are an increasingly common sight in rural areas of this country. Are factory-farm operations healthy for their neighbors, for people in other parts of the country, and the environment? Many people think that these operations damage our air and water more than small family farms.

One problem with factory farming is the groundwater in the Midwest that has been contaminated by toxic waste. In addition, air quality produces bad-smelling and sometimes dangerous gases that people living near a CAFO have to breathe. When a factory farm's neighbors complain may not be able to close the operation. The reason is because most factory farms have powerful corporate backers.

Not everyone is angry about the CAFO situation; consumers get a short-term benefit from a large supply of pork, beef, and chicken that is cheaper than family farms can raise. However, the more people know about factory farms, the less interest in supporting their farming practices.

15.1 Identifying conjunctions

Underline the coordinating and subordinating conjunctions as well as the conjunctive adverbs in each of the following sentences. (See *EasyWriter*, pp. 90–94.) Example:

> **We used sleeping bags <u>even though</u> the cabin had both sheets <u>and</u> blankets.**

1. The shops along the waterfront were open, but business was slow.

2. The colt walked calmly, for he seemed to know he would win the race.

3. Pokey is an outside cat; nevertheless, she greets me at the front door each night as I arrive home.

4. When we arrived at the pond, we saw many children playing there.

5. Although I live in a big city, my neighborhood has enough trees and raccoons to make me feel as though I live in the suburbs.

6. Exhausted men and women worked the pumps until their arms ached.

7. Because the downtown area has many successful businesses, people still want to live inside the city limits.

15.2 Combining sentences with coordination

Using the principles of coordination to signal equal importance or to create special emphasis, combine and revise the following twelve short sentences into several longer and more effective ones. Add or delete words as necessary. (See *EasyWriter*, pp. 90–94.)

The bull-riding arena was fairly crowded. The crowd made no impression on me. I had made a decision. It was now time to prove myself. I was scared. I walked to the entry window. I placed my money on the counter. The clerk held up a Stetson hat filled with slips of paper. I reached in. I picked one. The slip held the number of the bull I was to ride. I headed

toward the stock corral.

15.3 Writing sentences with subordination

Combine each of the following sets of sentences into one sentence
that uses subordination to signal the relationships among ideas. Add
or delete words as necessary. (See *EasyWriter,* pp. 92–94.) Example:

> **The bus swerved to avoid hitting a dog.**
> **It narrowly missed a car.**
> **The car was in the bus driver's blind spot.**
>
> When the bus swerved to avoid hitting a dog, it narrowly missed a car
> that was in the bus driver's blind spot.

1. The scenery in the park is beautiful.

   The mountains have caps of snow.

   The lakes are deep and full of fish.

   The pastures are green.

   It is an ideal spot to spend spring break.

2. I spent a long night on a sleep sofa.

   I was at my parents' house.

   The sleep sofa has an uncomfortably thin mattress with a hard metal

   bar beneath it.

3. Al Franken wrote a book about conservatives in American media.

   Fox News filed a lawsuit to stop publication of the book.

   The lawsuit was thrown out of court.

   The book became a best-seller.

4. I walked into the shelter.

   Men, women, and children were slumped against the wall.

   Shopping carts containing families' belongings lay on their sides.

5. We had dug a seventy-foot ditch.

   My boss would pour gravel into the ditch.

   I would level the gravel with a shovel.

15.4 Using coordination and subordination

Revise the following paragraph, using coordination and subordination where appropriate to clarify the relationships between ideas. (See *EasyWriter,* pp. 90–94.)

Wasabi is a root. It originally came from Japan. Wasabi is prized as a spice. It can cost as much as $100 per pound. It is related to horseradish. Wasabi has the same sinus-clearing effect that horseradish has. It grows in icy mountain streams. Wasabi is difficult to grow on farms. American farmers are trying to perfect techniques for growing wasabi in this country. One Californian has invested in expensive technology for his wasabi farm. His name is Roy Carver. He is the largest producer of wasabi outside of Japan. People have tried to sneak onto his farm to see how he grows wasabi. He now keeps the location of his wasabi farm a closely guarded secret.

16.1 Eliminating unnecessary words and phrases

Make each of the following sentences clear and concise by eliminating unnecessary words and phrases and by making additions or revisions as needed. (See *EasyWriter,* pp. 94–96.) Example:

The ~~incredible, unbelievable~~ feats that Houdini performed amazed and ~~astounded~~ all of his audiences ~~who came to see him.~~

1. Harry Houdini, whose real birth name was Ehrich Weiss, made the claim that he had been born in Appleton, Wisconsin, but in actual fact he was born into the world in Budapest, Hungary.

2. Shortly after Houdini's birth, his family moved to Appleton, where his father served as the one and only rabbi in Appleton at that point in time.

3. Houdini gained fame as a really great master escape artist.

4. His many numerous escapes included getting out of a giant sealed envelope without tearing it and walking out of jail cells that were said to be supposedly escape-proof.

5. Before his untimely early death, Houdini told his brother to burn and destroy all papers describing how Houdini's illusions worked.

6. Clearly, it is quite obvious that Houdini did not want anyone at all to know his hidden secrets.

7. Part of the explanation for Houdini's escape artistry lies in the fact that his physique was in absolutely peak physical condition.

8. Houdini's tremendous control over almost every single individual muscle allowed him to contort his body into seemingly impossible positions.

9. After his mother's death, Houdini grew interested in spiritualism until he discovered that the mediums who were the people running the séances were frauds trying to do nothing more than bilk and cheat their customers.

10. On his deathbed, Houdini promised his wife that he would try and attempt to make contact with her from beyond the grave, but so far, he has never been able to get in touch yet.

16.2   Revising for conciseness

Revise the following paragraph so that each sentence is as concise as possible. Combine or divide sentences if necessary. (See *EasyWriter*, pp. 94–96.)

At the present time, one of the most serious problems that faces
Americans in the area of public policy is the increasing rise in the cost of
health care, which has occurred over an extended period of time. One major
aspect of the severe crisis in health care costs is that more and more
expensive medical technology is being developed and marketed to doctors
and hospitals. Even hospitals that are small in size want the latest kind of
diagnostic device. The high cost of this expensive equipment is passed on to
consumers, who are the patients. It is then passed on to insurance companies.
Therefore, many employers are charging their employees more for health
insurance because they themselves are having to pay higher and higher
premiums. Others are reducing the employees' coverage to a significant
extent. Meanwhile, almost forty million Americans suffer from the condition
of a lack of any health insurance. In the event that they have an illness or an
injury, they must go to a hospital emergency room. In large cities, emergency
rooms are now being overwhelmed today by people seeking treatment for
everything from a minor cold to a life-threatening gunshot wound.

17.1　Creating parallel words or phrases

Complete the following sentences, using parallel words or phrases
in each case. (See *EasyWriter,* pp. 96–98.) Example:

> The wise politician _promises the possible_ , _effects the unavoidable_ ,
>
> and _accepts the inevitable_ .

1. My favorite pastimes include _____ , _____ ,

   and _____ .

2. I want not only _____ but also _____ .

3. My motto is _____ , _____ , and

   _____ .

4. I told my younger sister _____ and

   _____ .

5. _____ , _____ , and _____

   are activities my grandparents enjoy.

6. When he got his promotion, he _____ , _____ ,

   and _____ .

7. You should _____ , _____ , or

   _____ before you invite six guests for dinner.

8. We must either _____ or _____ .

9. Graduates find that the job market _____ ,

   _____ , and _____ .

10. The contract required the workers _____ and

    _____ .

17.2 Revising sentences for parallelism

Revise the following sentences to eliminate any errors in parallel
structure. (See *EasyWriter*, pp. 96–98.) Example:

> **Pérez Prado's orchestra was famous for playing irresistible rhythms**
> turning
> **and ~~because it turned~~ the mambo into a new dance craze.**
>   ^

1. The latest dance steps and wearing festive party clothes were necessi-
   ties for many teenagers in the 1950s.

2. Many people in this country remember how they danced to the mambo
   music of the 1950s and listening to that era's Latin bands.

3. Older dancers may recall Rosemary Clooney, Perry Como, and Ruth
   Brown singing mambo numbers and Pérez Prado's band had a huge hit,
   "Cherry Pink and Apple Blossom White."

4. Growing up near Havana and a student of classical piano, Pérez Prado loved Cuban music.

5. Pérez Prado wanted not only to play Cuban music but also he wanted to combine it with elements of jazz.

6. Playing piano in Havana nightclubs, arranging music for a Latin big band, and the jam sessions he joined with the band's guitarists gave him the idea for a new kind of music.

7. The result was a new dance phenomenon: mambo music was born, and Pérez Prado, who became known as "King of the Mambo."

8. Prado conducted his orchestra with hand-waving, head and shoulder movements, and by kicking his feet high in the air.

9. His recordings feature syncopated percussion, wailing trumpets, and Prado shouted rhythmically.

10. Pérez Prado, innovative and a great musician, died in 1989.

17.3 Revising for parallelism and supplying necessary words

Revise the following paragraph to maintain parallelism where it exists and to supply all words necessary for clarity, grammar, and idiom in parallel structures. (See *EasyWriter*, pp. 96–98.)

Family gatherings for events such as weddings, holidays, and going on vacation are supposed to be happy occasions, but for many people, getting together with family members causes tremendous stress. Everyone hopes to share warm memories and for a picture-perfect family event. Unfortunately, the reality may include an uncle who makes offensive remarks, a critical mother, or anger at a spouse who doesn't lift a finger to help. Neither difficult relatives nor when things go wrong will necessarily ruin a big family gathering, however. The trick is to plan for problems and being able to adapt. Family members who are not flexible, not pleasant to be around, or willing to do their part will always be a problem for their relatives. However, people who try to make a family gathering a success will almost always either be able to enjoy the event or laugh about it later.

18.1 Revising for verb tense and mood

Revise any of the following sentences in which you find unnecessary shifts in verb tense or in mood. If a sentence is correct as written, write C. (See *EasyWriter*, pp. 98–99.) Examples:

The doctor examined six patients, but she only ~~washes~~ _washed_ her hands four times.

Scrub with soap for ten to fifteen seconds and ~~you should~~ rinse thoroughly.

1. Over 150 years ago, a Hungarian doctor discovered that doctors who deliver babies and did not thoroughly wash their hands often spread a deadly infection to new mothers.

2. Today, we know better. It is common knowledge that unclean hands transmit germs.

3. Most people learn as children that keeping their hands clean is very important. However, sometimes they forgot this lesson in later life.

4. All health care workers should know that they had to keep their hands clean.

5. Unfortunately, a new study indicates that a high percentage of busy health care workers did not wash their hands often enough.

6. Hand-washing can be repetitive, time consuming, and boring, but it should be crucial to patient safety in every hospital.

7. Approximately 5 percent of the patients who were admitted to hospitals this year will get an infection there. Some of those infections may be deadly.

8. The bacteria that cause these infections could not travel through the air. They require physical contact to move from place to place.

9. If all hospital workers were to wash their hands regularly, fewer infections travel from patient to patient.

10. Wash your hands frequently, and you should follow these instructions even if your skin gets dry.

18.2 Eliminating shifts in voice and point of view

Revise each of the following sentences to eliminate an unnecessary shift in voice or point of view. (See *EasyWriter*, p. 99.) Example:

The dancers performed on a low stage as a jig ~~was played by a~~ fiddler played a ~~fiddler.~~

1. If one visits the local art museum, you will find recent prints by Greg Pfarr on display.

2. I liked the sense of individualism, the crowd yelling for you, and the feeling that I was in command.

3. The police sent protesters to a distant "free speech zone," but supporters were allowed to stand along the motorcade route.

4. When someone says "roommate" to a high school senior bound for college, thoughts of no privacy and potential fights are conjured up.

5. The physician moves the knee around to observe the connections of the cartilage and ligaments, and a fluid is injected into the joint.

6. We knew that you shouldn't walk across the railroad trestle, but we went ahead anyway.

7. When the snapping turtle attacked me and Jake, Jake was bitten on the hand, but I swam away.

8. The roses were gathered by Lionel, and then he arranged them.

9. Sea anemones thrive in coastal tide pools, but it cannot survive outside the water for very long.

10. Suddenly we heard an explosion of wings off to our right, and you could see a hundred or more ducks lifting off from the water.

18.3 Eliminating shifts between direct and indirect discourse

To eliminate the shifts between direct and indirect discourse in the following sentences, put the direct discourse into indirect form. (See *EasyWriter*, pp. 99–100.) Example:

        states   his
Steven Pinker ~~stated~~ that ~~my~~ book is meant for people who use
           ^   ^

language and respect it.

1. Richard Rodriguez acknowledges that intimacy was not created by a language; "it is created by intimates."

2. She said that during a semester abroad, "I really missed all my friends."

3. The bewildered neighbor asked him, "What the heck he thought he was doing on the roof?"

4. Loren Eiseley feels an urge to join the birds in their soundless flight, but in the end he understands that he cannot, and "I was, after all, only a man."

5. The instructor told us, "Please read the next two stories before the next class" and that she might give us a quiz on them.

18.4 Eliminating shifts in tone and diction

Revise each of the following sentences to eliminate shifts in tone and diction. (See *EasyWriter*, p. 100.) Example:

How do I
Excuse me. ~~In which direction should I proceed to~~ **get to the mall?**

1. I am astounded by the number of emails I receive each day trying to flog meds to me.

2. The Chinese invented noodles, though lots of people think that the Italians must have come up with that bright idea.

3. Most commuters keep to a predictable schedule, hopping a bus or train to the 'burbs at the same time each night.

4. The Guggenheim exhibit of African works of art, often misunderstood and undervalued by Western art historians, is a heck of a show.

5. After she had yanked little William out of the busy street by the strap of his overalls, she tendered a verbal rebuke that left both the child and his mother sniffling.

Punctuation/Mechanics

19.1 Using a comma to set off introductory elements

In the following sentences, add any commas that are needed after the introductory element. If no comma is necessary, write C. (See *EasyWriter,* p. 102.) Example:

> **Using technology in new ways, scientists are working on an electronic nose.**

1. Although the idea of an electronic nose may sound odd such a nose would have many uses.

2. In the past doctors recognized some ailments by a characteristic odor.

3. Having strep throat causes a person to give off a particular scent that a trained nose can identify.

4. Of course throat cultures can also spot strep throat, but they take time.

5. When a strep infection is identified immediately by its smell a patient can get immediate treatment.

6. Someday electronic noses may be perfected.

7. Along with this technological advance is likely to come disbelief that electronic noses could be useful.

8. Naturally people may appreciate the idea of using electronic noses to avoid invasive medical procedures.

9. But if electronic noses get more sensitive they could be used for tasks human noses find unpleasant.

10. Unable to judge whether smells are delectable or nauseating an electronic nose might be a valuable aid to a human one.

19.2 Using a comma in compound sentences

Use a comma and a coordinating conjunction (*and, but, or, for, nor, so,* or *yet*) to combine each of the following pairs of sentences into one sentence. Delete or rearrange words if necessary. (See *EasyWriter,* p. 103.) Example:

The phrase *test-tube baby* is rarely used today. In vitro fertilization is common.

1. Treatments for infertility become more promising each year. In vitro fertilization has helped many people have children.

2. Over two decades ago, fertility treatments were a little-explored field. The first "test-tube baby" astonished the world.

3. *In vitro* means "in glass." In vitro fertilization does indeed take place in a lab dish.

4. A scientist combines an egg cell and a sperm cell. An embryo forms when the egg cell begins to divide.

5. The embryo that grows is returned to the mother's uterus. The process of growing to viability cannot take place entirely in a laboratory.

6. The procedure requires scientific intervention. The parents of a "test-tube baby" have a child that is biologically theirs.

7. Before in vitro fertilization, would-be parents might have given up on the idea of having children. They might have spent years trying to adopt a child.

8. In vitro fertilization has helped many people have children. It is expensive.

9. There are other, newer methods of helping infertile couples. In vitro fertilization no longer astonishes the public.

10. The first "test-tube baby," who was born in England, was a celebrity. Today, children whose parents used in vitro fertilization are quite common.

19.3 Recognizing restrictive and nonrestrictive elements

First, underline the restrictive or the nonrestrictive elements in the following sentences. Then, use commas to set off the nonrestrictive elements in any of the sentences that contain such elements. (See *EasyWriter,* pp. 103–6.) Example:

My only novel, *The Family Kurasch*, is out of print.

1. Anyone who is fourteen years old faces strong peer pressure every day.

2. Embalming is a technique that preserves a cadaver.

3. The word *chortle* which was invented by Lewis Carroll is a combination of the words *chuckle* and *snort.*

4. My favorite pastime reading Web logs often prevents me from getting enough sleep or doing all my homework.

5. The president elected for a six-year term acts as head of state.

6. Thurgood Marshall the first African American to serve on the U.S. Supreme Court died in 1993.

7. Houses made of wood can often survive earthquakes.

8. Trey Parker and Matt Stone who created *South Park* met as college students in Colorado.

9. The man who rescued her puppy won her eternal gratitude.

10. The tornado which had spared Waterville leveled Douglastown.

19.4 Using commas to set off items in a series

In the following sentences, add any commas that are needed to set off words, phrases, or clauses in a series. If no comma is needed, write C. (See *EasyWriter*, p. 106.) Example:

The waiter brought water, menus, and an attitude.

1. From his new job, Jake wanted money prestige and a challenge, in that order.

2. I am looking forward to turning eighteen being able to vote and perhaps serving in the military.

3. The spider's orange body resembles a colored dot amidst eight long black legs.

4. The moon circles the earth the earth revolves around the sun and the sun is just one star among many in the Milky Way galaxy.

5. The ball sailed over the fence across the road and through the Wilsons' window.

6. Ellen is an accomplished freelance writer.

7. They found employment in truck driving farming and mining.

8. The firm's quiet pleasant excessively polite public relations executives made everyone a little nervous.

9. James Joyce wrote novels short stories and poems.

10. Superficial observation does not provide accurate insight into people's lives—how they feel what they believe in how they respond to others.

19.5 Using commas to set off parenthetical and transitional expressions, contrasting elements, interjections, direct address, and tag questions

Revise each of the following sentences, using commas to set off parenthetical and transitional expressions, contrasting elements, interjections, words used in direct address, and tag questions. (See *EasyWriter*, p. 107.) Example:

Ladies and gentlemen, thank you for your attention.
  ^

1. Hey stop ogling that construction worker!

2. Madame President I move to adjourn the meeting.

3. Now we can stitch the seam right?

4. The West in fact has become solidly Republican in presidential elections.

5. Last year I am sorry to say six elms had to be destroyed.

6. Captain Kirk I'm a doctor not a madman.

7. The celebration will alas conclude all too soon.

8. One must consider the society as a whole not just its parts.

9. Her friends did not know about her illness did they?

10. Mary announced, "Kids I want you to clean your rooms not make a

    bigger mess."

19.6 Using commas with dates, addresses, and quotations

Revise each of the following sentences, using commas appropriately with dates, addresses and place-names, and quotations. If no comma is needed in a sentence, write C. (See *EasyWriter*, pp. 107–8.) Example:

The wine store's original location was 2373 Broadway, New York
  ^
City.

1. James Baldwin wrote in 1953 "This world is white no longer, and it will never be white again."

2. Who remarked that "youth is wasted on the young"?

3. "The public be damned!" William Henry Vanderbilt was reported to have said. "I'm working for my stockholders."

4. "Who can match the desperate humorlessness of the adolescent who thinks he is the first to discover seriousness?", asks P. J. Kavanaugh.

5. MLA headquarters are at 26 Broadway New York New York 10004.

6. The ship was hit by two torpedoes on May 7 1915 and sank in minutes.

7. "Neat people are lazier and meaner than sloppy people" according to Suzanne Britt.

19.7 Eliminating unnecessary and inappropriate commas

Revise each of the following sentences, deleting unnecessary commas. If a sentence contains no unnecessary commas, write C. (See *EasyWriter*, pp. 109–10.) Example:

Insomniacs are people, who have a hard time sleeping soundly.

1. Contrary to popular belief, insomnia is not simply a matter, of being unable to sleep well at night.

2. Insomniacs do indeed wake up at night, but, studies have demonstrated that they also have trouble napping during the day.

3. Why can't insomniacs sleep soundly at night, or nap when they are tired?

4. In many cases, insomniacs suffer, from anxiety.

5. Doctors and sleep researchers, have long considered anxiety to be a common result of getting too little sleep.

6. However, recent studies indicate that anxiety contributes to sleeplessness, not the other way around.

7. Therapies to help insomniacs, include behavior modification and sleeping pills.

8. Sleep therapists recommend, going to bed at the same time every night, not watching television in bed, and not reading in bed.

9. Restless, disturbed, sleep habits are certainly irritating, but are they also, bad for an insomniac's health?

10. Although tired people are more dangerous drivers, and less productive workers, no one knows for certain, if insomnia can actually make them sick.

20.1 Using semicolons to link clauses

Combine each of the following pairs of sentences into one sentence by using a semicolon. (See *EasyWriter,* pp. 110–11.) Example:

                                     ; *meet*
Take the bus to Henderson Street, ~~Meet~~ me under the clock.

1. City life offers many advantages. In many ways, however, life in a small town is much more pleasant.

2. Teenagers today don't spend all their time on the telephone. Instead, they go online and send each other instant messages.

3. Voltaire was concerned about the political implications of his skepticism. He warned his friends not to discuss atheism in front of the servants.

4. The unwanted package arrived C.O.D. I politely refused to pay the charges.

5. Current celebrities don't have to make fools of themselves on reality television shows. Former celebrities jump at the chance.

6. Pittsburgh was once notorious for its smoke and grime. Today, its skies and streets are cleaner than those of many other American cities.

7. I used to see nothing but woods when I looked out my back window. The view was nothing like it is now, a treeless expanse of new houses.

8. Establishing your position in an office is an important task. Your profile will mold your relationships with other staff members.

9. *Propaganda* is defined as the spread of ideas to further a cause. Therefore, *propaganda* and *advertisement* are synonyms.

10. Florida's mild winter climate is ideal for bicycling. In addition, the terrain is very flat.

20.2 Eliminating misused semicolons

Revise each of the following sentences to correct the misuse of semi-colons. (See *EasyWriter*, p. 112.) Example:

The new system would encourage high school students to take more academic courses/, thus strengthening college preparation.

1. We must find a plan to provide decent health care; a necessity in today's life.

2. Verbal scores have decreased by more than fifty-four points; while math scores have decreased by more than thirty-six.

3. For four glorious but underpaid weeks; I'll be working in Yosemite this summer.

4. Finally, I found her at the Humane Society; a beautiful shepherd-collie mix who likes children and plays well with cats.

5. If the North had followed up its victory at Gettysburg more vigorously; the Civil War might have ended sooner.

6. He left a large estate; which was used to endow a scholarship fund.

7. Some gardeners want; low-maintenance plants, limited grass to mow, and low water usage.

8. You can't take your ball and go home; just because you think you'll lose the game.

9. After school; many fourteen-year-olds head to the mall; where they spend the rest of the day.

10. The speech made sense to some observers; but not to me.

21.1 Using periods appropriately

Revise each of the following items, inserting periods in the appropriate places and eliminating any inappropriate punctuation. If a sentence is correct, write C. (See *EasyWriter*, p. 113.) Example:

Dr. Sarah Blaffer Hrdy has been studying the maternal instinct in
   ^
humans and other animals.
       ^

1. Dr Hrdy, an anthropologist, has studied primate motherhood for many years.

2. She has raised disturbing questions about why parents sometimes kill their offspring?

3. Parents since the Neolithic period of 10,000 BCE have delayed naming infants or otherwise committing to raising them until a few days after birth.

4. Human parents, even in recent centuries, may actively or passively have limited their children's chances to grow up!

5. Dr Hrdy believes that parents may commit infanticide in order to give their other children a better chance

6. The term "parent-offspring conflict" was coined by Robert Trivers, PhD?

7. The popular view of motherhood is that mothers always love their children unconditionally

8. Many mothers are indeed willing to put up with a great deal from their children, from 2.00 am feedings through requests for college tuition.

9. Dr Hrdy asks whether the "maternal instinct" is really instinctive?

10. Describing a mother's crime against her child as "inhuman" is neither accurate nor helpful in preventing future tragedies!

21.2 Using question marks appropriately

Revise each of the following sentences, adding question marks, substituting question marks for other punctuation where appropriate, and removing inappropriately placed question marks. Some sentences do not require any question marks; for those sentences, write C. (See *EasyWriter,* p. 114.) Example:

She asked the travel agent, "What is the air fare to Greece?"

1. The reporter asked whether the president could explain his proposal in simpler terms?

2. "Can I play this" asked Manuel.

3. Did you just say, "What time is it?"?

4. "How long are we supposed to wait for Sara," wondered Erin?

5. Who said, "Give me liberty, or give me death?"

6. She asked the officer if she could call her lawyer.

7. "Have you heard the one about the tourist and the barber," he asked.

8. What do you think of your new office? your new salary?

21.3 Using exclamation points appropriately

Revise each of the following sentences, adding or deleting exclamation points as necessary and removing any other inappropriate punctuation that you find. (See *EasyWriter,* p. 114.) Example:

Look out, the tide is coming in fast.

1. The defendant stood up in the witness box and shouted, "I didn't do it. You've got to believe me."

2. Oh, no. We've lost the house.

3. The child cried, "Ouch" as her mother pulled off the bandage!

4. "Go! Go! Go!," roared the crowd as the quarterback sped toward the end zone.

5. "This is ridiculous," sputtered the diner as the waiter brought the wrong order again!

22.1 Using apostrophes to signal possession

Complete each of the following sentences by inserting *'s* or an apostrophe alone to form the possessive case of the italicized words. (See *EasyWriter,* pp. 115–16.) Example:

Many Internet scare stories are nothing but old *wives'* tales.

1. Internet rumors circulate widely because of *people* good intentions.

2. Recipients who pass on messages want everyone to hear about a *child* inspiring fight against cancer or about some dangerous drug, product, or disease.

3. The *Internet* power to inform is great, but so is its power to play tricks on unsuspecting people.

4. A *hoax* creators count on *recipients* kind hearts and concern for the well-being of their families and friends.

5. *Consumers* fears fuel some of the Internet medical scares.

6. Have you heard the one about how a *deodorant* ingredients supposedly clog your pores and cause cancer?

7. Another scare warned that sugar substitutes caused the *body* immune system to malfunction.

8. Some of these scares are probably intended to damage certain *corporations* reputations by spreading rumors about products.

9. Others, like the one about checking your toilet seat to be sure it has not become a deadly *spider* hiding place, probably begin as jokes.

10. The *Internet* speed has allowed such anonymous rumors to spread more rapidly than anyone would have thought possible twenty years ago.

22.2 Using apostrophes appropriately

Revise each of the following sentences so that it uses apostrophes appropriately. (See *EasyWriter*, p. 116.) Example:

> That's
> ~~That is~~ the classical music used in the movie *Elvira Madigan*.
> ^

1. She is his favorite person, but he is not her's.

2. I cant believe you have'nt started the paper yet; it's due tomorrow morning.

3. Its hard to identify the best new novelist of the decade.

4. That guy whose been giving you a ride after work called at about nine o'clock.

5. For the test youll be taking on Monday, youre required to have a No. 2 pencil.

6. The clothes that Im washing now did'nt really get too dirty.

7. The caller says he has been waiting an hour for his pizza's, but we don't have any record of his order.

8. The distributor says that your order has not received it's approval from the business office.

9. It's true that a snake can shed it's own skin and can swallow much of its prey whole.

10. That cat of your's is nothing but trouble.

23.1 Using quotation marks to signal direct quotation

In the following sentences, add quotation marks each time someone else's exact words are being used. Some sentences do not require quotation marks; mark correct sentences C. (See *EasyWriter,* pp. 117–19.) Example:

> **"   "**
> **Your phone's ringing! yelled Phil from the end of the hall.**

1. Although many people believe that Rick says Play it again, Sam, in *Casablanca,* those exact words do not appear in the film.

2. After a tornado ripped through her house, a tearful Indiana woman said she had nothing left.

3. The county employment office's annual summary states that the current unemployment rate is 37 percent lower than it was five years ago.

4. To repeat their words, we have turned the corner.

5. Call me Ishmael is the first sentence of novelist Herman Melville's *Moby Dick.*

6. Most people like to think of themselves as open-minded and flexible enough to change when the circumstances demand.

7. After repeating I can't hear you with her fingers stuck in her ears, Hannah ran to her room and slammed the door.

8. I could not believe the condition of my hometown, he wrote.

9. Keep your opinions to yourselves, Dad muttered as he served the lumpy oatmeal.

10. Is the computer plugged in? the technical support operator asked, prompting Harry to snarl, Yes, I'm not a complete idiot.

23.2 Using quotation marks for titles and definitions

Revise each of the following sentences, using quotation marks appropriately to signal titles and definitions. (See *EasyWriter*, pp. 119–20.) Example:

> **The Chinese American businessman surprised his guest by using the Hebrew word *shalom*, which means "peace."**

1. The slogan for the Center for a New American Dream is appropriately simple: More Fun, Less Stuff.

2. My dictionary defines *isolation* as the quality or state of being alone.

3. Two *ER* episodes, Chaos Theory and Freefall, featured Dr. Romano having a run-in with a helicopter.

4. Kowinski uses the term *mallaise* to mean physical and psychological disturbances caused by mall contact.

5. In Flannery O'Connor's short story *Revelation,* colors symbolize passion, violence, sadness, and even God.

6. "The little that is known about gorillas certainly makes you want to know more," writes Alan Moorehead in his essay A Most Forgiving Ape.

7. The British, the guide told us, knit sweaters for their teapots.

8. If you had ever had Stairway to Heaven running through your head for four days straight, you would not like Led Zeppelin either.

9. Big Bill, a section of Dos Passos's book *U.S.A.*, opens with a birth.

10. Amy Lowell challenges social conformity in her poem Patterns.

23.3 Using quotation marks appropriately

Revise each of the following sentences, deleting quotation marks used inappropriately, moving those placed incorrectly, and changing wording as necessary. (See *EasyWriter*, pp. 117–21.) Example:

Do advertisements /really/ have something to teach us about our culture?

1. Cable channels such as "Nickelodeon" include what they term "classic" commercials as part of the programming.

2. Television commercials have frequently used "popular" songs as an effective way to connect their product with good feelings in consumers' minds.

3. Many middle-aged Americans still associate the wee-oo sound of the theremin from the Beach Boys' Good Vibrations with images of beach-goers enjoying orange soft drinks.

4. The strategy of using hit songs in commercials can "backfire" when the listeners don't like the song or like it too much to think of it as an advertising "jingle."

5. Many aging baby boomers were disturbed to hear "Beatles" songs being used to sell shoes.

6. The rights to many Beatles songs, such as "Revolution", are no longer controlled by the Beatles.

7. Sometimes advertisements contain songs that seem to have no connection at all to the products being "plugged."

8. Many Iggy Pop fans wonder what on earth his song Lust for Life has to do with taking an expensive ocean cruise.

9. Not surprisingly, the song's more peculiar lyrics, including Well, that's like hypnotizing chickens, are omitted from the cruise-line advertisements.

10. Do consumers love the songs of their youth so much that merely hearing a song in an "ad" will make them buy that car?

24.1 Using parentheses and brackets

Revise the following sentences, using parentheses and brackets correctly. Change any other punctuation in the sentences as needed. (See *EasyWriter,* pp. 121–23.) Example:

> **Many observers(and not just from right-wing media outlets) have**
> ^
> **argued that U.S. journalists are not doing a thorough job of present-**
> **ing political issues.**

1. The words *media elite* have been said so often usually by people who are themselves elite members of the media that the phrase has taken on a life of its own.

2. Are the media really elite, and are they really liberal, as talk-show regulars (Ann Coulter, for example argue)?

3. Media critic Eric Alterman has coined the term "so-called liberal media" [SCLM] because he believes that the media have been intimidated by criticism.

4. An article in the *Journal of Communication* discussing the outcome of recent U.S. elections explained that "claiming the media are liberally

biased perhaps has become a core rhetorical strategy" used by conservatives, qtd. in Alterman 14.

5. Some progressive groups (including Fairness and Accuracy in Reporting (FAIR)) keep track of media coverage of political issues and campaigns.

6. However, liberals are not the only media watchdogs: right-wing organizations, including Accuracy in Media, (AIM) also closely examine the way political stories are reported.

7. The nonpartisan Campaign Desk Web site [sponsored by the *Columbia Journalism Review*] was dedicated to tracking media coverage of the 2004 presidential election.

8. According to the site's home page, the purpose of Campaign Desk was "to straighten and deepen campaign coverage" as a resource for voters (most of whom rely on media coverage to make decisions about the candidates.)

9. Is truly objective coverage of hot-button issues and political candidates, (whether Republicans or Democrats,) ever possible?

10. And can we forget that as media consumers, we have an obligation to be an informed electorate (even though it's easy to pay attention only to the news that reinforces our own beliefs.)?

24.2   Using dashes

Revise the following sentences so that dashes are used correctly. If the sentence is correct as written, write C. (See *EasyWriter*, pp. 123–24.) Example:

In some states California, for example banks are no longer allowed to charge ATM users an additional fee for withdrawing money.

1. Many consumers accept the fact that they have to pay additional fees for services such as bank machines if they don't want to pay, they don't have to use the service.

2. Nevertheless, — extra charges seem to be added to more and more services all the time.

3. Some of the charges are ridiculous why should hotels charge guests a fee for making a toll-free telephone call?

4. The hidden costs of service fees are irritating people feel that their bank accounts are being nibbled to death.

5. But some of the fees consumers are asked to pay — are more than simply irritating.

6. The "convenience charges" — that people have to pay when buying show tickets by telephone — are often a substantial percentage of the cost of the ticket.

7. If ticket buyers don't want to pay these "convenience charges" and who does? they must buy their tickets at the box office.

8. Finally, there are government fees that telephone companies and other large corporations are required to pay.

9. Telephone companies routinely pass these fees used to ensure Internet access to remote areas and schools along to their customers, implying that the government expects consumers to pay.

10. Many consumers are not aware that the government requires the corporations—not the general public—to pay these fees.

24.3 Using colons

Insert a colon in each of the following items that needs one. If the sentence is correct as written, write C. (See *EasyWriter,* p. 124.) Example:

> **Some fans of the *Star Wars* films have created a new online version of *Episode I : The Phantom Menace* that deletes all of the scenes with Jar Jar Binks.**

1. Gandhi urged four rules tell the truth even in business, adopt more sanitary habits, abolish caste and religious divisions, and learn English.

2. Solid vocal technique is founded on the correct use of head position, diaphragm control, muscle relaxation, and voice placement.

3. Another example is taken from Psalm 139 16.

4. The sonnet's structure is effective in revealing the speaker's message love has changed his life and ended his depression.

5. The article "Slim Pickings Looking beyond Ephedra" explains that few legal drugs promote weight loss.

6. Even more important was what money represented success, prestige, and power.

7. Voters rejected the school budget increase by a 2,1 margin, leaving school officials wondering how to cope with classroom overcrowding.

8. Education can alleviate problems such as poverty, poor health, and the energy shortage.

9. Doug and I both asked ourselves the same question "What happens if one of us gets sick?"

10. Reviewers agree that Halwani's book possesses these traits readability, intelligence, and usefulness.

24.4 Using ellipses

Read the following passage. Then assume that the underlined portions have been left out in a reprinting of the passage. Indicate how you would use ellipses to indicate those deletions. (See *EasyWriter*, pp. 125–26.) Example:

> . . .
> Saving money is difficult ~~for young people in entry-level positions~~,
> but it is important.

Should young people <u>who are just getting started in their careers</u> think about saving for retirement? Those who begin to save in their twenties <u>are making a wise financial decision. They</u> are putting away money that can earn compound interest for decades. Even if they save only a hundred dollars a month, and even if they stop saving when they hit age thirty-five, the total forty years later will be impressive. <u>On the other hand,</u> people who wait until they are fifty to begin saving will have far less money put aside at the age of sixty-five. People who wait too long may face an impoverished retirement <u>unless they are able to save thousands of dollars each month.</u> Of course, no one knows how long he or she will live, but saving is a way of gambling on reaching retirement. Difficult as it may be to think about being sixty-five or seventy years old, young people should plan ahead.

24.5 Reviewing punctuation marks

Correct the punctuation in the following sentences. If the punctuation is already correct, write C. (See *EasyWriter*, pp. 102–26.) Example:

> Children/who are too young to speak/are often frustrated because
> they cannot communicate their wishes.

1. Many American parents are willing to try almost anything prenatal music, infant flash cards, you name it to help their children succeed.

2. Some parental efforts do help children, for instance, children whose parents read to them are more likely to enjoy books.

3. Other schemes to make babies smarter, such as those based on the so-called *Mozart effect,* apparently don't make much difference.

4. A new idea that is "popular" with many parents of young children is sign language.

5. Researcher Joseph Garcia an expert in child development and in American Sign Language noticed that hearing babies with deaf parents often learned sign language before they could speak.

6. By sixteen to eighteen months, most children are able to speak simple words, and make themselves understood.

7. However, babies can communicate simple ideas to their parents starting at about eight months, if the infants learn signs.

8. Garcia showed that parents could easily teach their children signs for words such as please, more, sleepy, and hungry.

9. Garcia wrote a book called "Sign with Your Baby."

10. Not surprisingly, parents bought the book, (and then the video,) and now sign-language classes for small children are easy to find.

11. Parents who go to signing classes with their infants and toddlers hope for a good outcome; better communication between parent and child and less frustration for both.

12. A study by California researchers found that seven-year-olds earned slightly higher IQ scores if they had learned to sign as infants.

13. It's not surprising that this studys results fueled the demand for more toddler sign-language classes.

14. The researchers who developed the study said that the best reason for parents to sign with their children was to allow the children "to communicate what they need and see".

15. One researcher, Dr Elizabeth Bates, told the "New York Times" that the hand movements that small children can learn are really gestures, not proper sign language.

16. Others contend that the childrens' hand movements stand for concepts so the movements are sign language.

17. Some parents fear that a child who learns to communicate by signs will have little incentive to speak researchers have found no evidence of this effect.

18. In fact children who can use sign language are often especially eager to learn how to speak.

19. Although signing appears to have some benefits for the children who learn it not everyone feels that parents need to rush out to attend a class.

20. Any activity that gets parents to spend more time communicating with their children probably has it's benefits.

25.1 Capitalizing

Capitalize words as needed in the following sentences. (See *Easy-Writer*, pp. 127–29.) Example:

> T S E   T W   L   F
> ~~T. S. Eliot~~, who wrote ~~the waste land~~, was an editor at ~~faber~~
>   F
> and ~~faber~~.

1. johnny depp appeared to be having a wonderful time playing captain jack sparrow in *pirates of the caribbean: the curse of the black pearl*.

2. the battle of lexington and concord was fought in april 1775.

3. i will cite the novels of vladimir nabokov, in particular *pnin* and *lolita.*

4. accepting an award for his score for the film *the high and the mighty*, dmitri tiomkin thanked beethoven, brahms, wagner, and strauss.

5. i wondered if my new levi's were faded enough.

6. we drove east over the hudson river on the tappan zee bridge.

7. senator trent lott was widely criticized after appearing to praise senator strom thurmond's segregationist past.

8. "bloody sunday" was a massacre of catholic protesters in derry, northern ireland, on january 30, 1972.

9. we had a choice of fast-food, chinese, or italian restaurants.

10. the town in the american south where i was raised had a statue of a civil war soldier in the center of main street.

26.1 Using abbreviations

Revise each of the following sentences to eliminate any abbreviations that would be inappropriate in academic writing. If a sentence is correct, write C. (See *EasyWriter*, pp. 130–31.) Example:

> international
> The ~~intl.~~ sport of belt sander racing began in a hardware store.
>   ^

1. Nielson Hardware in Point Roberts, WA, was the site of the world's first belt sander race in 1989.

2. The power tools, ordinarily used for sanding wood, are placed on a thirty-ft. track and plugged in; the sander to reach the end first wins.

3. Today, the International Belt Sander Drag Race Association (IBSDRA) sponsors tours of winning sanders, an international championship, and a Web site that sells IBSDRA T-shirts.

4. There are three divisions of belt sander races: the stock div., which races sanders right out of the box; the modified div., which allows any motor the owner wants to add; and the decorative div., which provides a creative outlet for sander owners.

5. An average race lasts two seconds, but the world champion modified sander raced the track in 1.52 secs.

6. The fastest sanders run on very coarse sandpaper—a no. sixteen grit is an excellent choice if it's available.

7. Stock sanders are usually widely available brands, e.g., Mikita or Bosch.

8. The S-B Power Tool Co. in Chicago, maker of Bosch sanders, allows participants to race its tools, but the co. does not underwrite races.

9. Another tool company, the Do It Best Corp. of Wayne, Ind., sponsors races across the U.S. and Canada.

10. No one knows what % of the nation's power tools have been used for this kind of entertainment.

26.2 Spelling out numbers and using figures

Revise the numbers in the following sentences as necessary for correctness and consistency. If a sentence is correct, write C. (See *EasyWriter*, pp. 131–32.) Example:

seventh   one

No correct answer choice was given for the ~~7th~~ question in part ~~1~~ of the test.

1. In the 35-to-44 age group, the risk is estimated to be about 1 in 2,500.

2. You could travel around the city for only 65 cents.

3. The amulet measured one and one-eighth by two and two-fifths inches.

4. Walker signed a three-year, $4.5-million contract.

5. The morning of September eleven, 2001, was cool and clear in New York City.

6. The parents considered twenty-five cents enough of an allowance for a five-year-old.

7. I drank 8 glasses of water, as the doctor had said, but then I had to get up 3 times during the night.

8. 307 miles long and 82 miles wide, the island offered little of interest.

9. Cable TV is now available to seventy-two percent of the population.

10. The department received 1,633 calls and forty-three letters.

27.1 Using italics

In each of the following sentences, underline any words that should be italicized, and circle any italicized words that should not be. If a title requires quotation marks instead of italicization, add them. (See *EasyWriter*, pp. 133–35.) Example:

The United States still abounds with regional speech — for example, many people in the Appalachians still use local words such as <u>crick</u> and <u>holler</u>.

1. *Regionalism*, a nineteenth-century literary movement, focused on the language and customs of people in areas of the country not yet affected by industrialization.

2. Regional writers produced some American classics, such as Mark Twain's Huckleberry Finn and James Fenimore Cooper's Last of the Mohicans.

3. Twain, not an admirer of Cooper's work, wrote a scathing essay about his predecessor called *The Literary Offenses of James Fenimore Cooper.*

4. Some of the most prolific regional writers were women such as Kate Chopin, who wrote her first collection of short stories, Bayou Folk, to help support her family.

5. The stories in *Bayou Folk*, such as the famous *Désirée's Baby*, focus on the natives of rural Louisiana.

6. Chopin also departed from regional works to explore women's experiences of marriage, as in her short piece, *The Story of an Hour.*

7. In Maine, Sarah Orne Jewett wrote sketches of rural life that appeared in the Atlantic Monthly.

8. She later turned these into a novel, Deephaven, which she hoped would "teach the world that country people were not . . . ignorant."

9. Her finest short story, *A White Heron*, and her celebrated novel *The Country of the Pointed Firs* also benefit from settings in Maine.

10. Many regional stories—Stephen Crane's *The Bride Comes to Yellow Sky* is a prime example—show the writer's concern that an isolated culture is in danger of disappearing.

28.1 Using hyphens in compounds and with prefixes

Insert hyphens as needed. A dictionary will help you with some items. If an item does not require a hyphen, write C. (See *EasyWriter*, pp. 135 – 36.) Example:

full͞ bodied wine
     ^

1. pro and anti-World Trade Organization marchers

2. thirty three

3. pre World War II

4. a politician who is fast talking

5. a hard working farmer

6. a what me worry look

7. deescalate

8. self guided

9. happily married couple

10. professor emeritus

28.2 Using hyphens appropriately

Insert or delete hyphens as needed. Use your dictionary if necessary. If a sentence is correct as printed, write C. (See *EasyWriter*, pp. 135 – 36.) Example:

The bleary͞ eyed student finally stopped fighting sleep and went to
          ^

bed.

1. The carpenter asked for a two pound bag of three quarter inch nails.

2. The name of the president elect had been announced an hour before the polls closed.

3. We urged him to be open minded and to temper his insensitive views.

4. Stress can lead to hypertension and ulcers.

5. Her dolllike features fooled many observers, but her competitors soon found that she had ice-cold blood and nerves-of-steel.

6. The ill fated antelope became the baboon's lunch.

7. The drum-beating and hand-clapping signaled that the parade was near.

8. The badly-wrapped sandwich oozed mustard and bits of soggy lettuce.

9. Suicide among teenagers has tripled in the past thirty five years.

10. One of Baryshnikov's favorite-dancers was Fred Astaire.

Language

30.1 Identifying stereotypes

Each of the following sentences stereotypes a person or a group of people. Underline the word or phrase that stereotypes the person or group. In each case, be ready to explain why the stereotype may be offensive, demeaning, or unfair. (See *EasyWriter*, pp. 141–42.) Example:

If you have trouble printing, ask a <u>computer geek</u> for help.

Assumes that all computer-savvy people are geeky, which is not the case.

1. The comedy show flopped because those rednecks in the audience don't understand satire.

2. Academics are extremely well paid, considering how few hours they actually teach.

3. Only a New Yorker could be so indifferent to the feelings of others.

4. I would never travel to France because everyone there hates Americans.

5. College kids need real-world experience.

6. Dropouts have trouble landing good jobs.

7. When we visit the nursing home, remember to treat the old folks with respect.

8. The ambulance chasers have clogged our court system.

30.2 Identifying and revising sexist language

The following excerpt is taken from the 1968 edition of Dr. Benjamin Spock's *Baby and Child Care*. Read it carefully, noting any language we might today consider sexist. Revise the passage, substituting non-sexist language as necessary. (See *EasyWriter*, p. 142.)

399. Feeling his oats. One year old is an exciting age. Your baby is changing in lots of ways—in his eating, in how he gets around, in what he wants to do and in how he feels about himself and other people. When he was little and helpless, you could put him where you wanted him, give him the playthings you thought suitable, feed him the foods you knew were best. Most of the time he was willing to let you be the boss, and took it all in good spirit. It's more complicated now that he is around a year old. He seems to realize that he's not meant to be a baby doll the rest of his life, that he's a human being with ideas and a will of his own.

When you suggest something that doesn't appeal to him, he feels he must assert himself. His nature tells him to. He just says No in words or actions, even about things that he likes to do. The psychologists call it "negativism"; mothers call it "that terrible No stage." But stop and think what would happen to him if he never felt like saying No. He'd become a robot, a mechanical man. You wouldn't be able to resist the temptation to boss him all the time, and he'd stop learning and developing. When he was old enough to go out into the world, to school and later to work, everybody else would take advantage of him, too. He'd never be good for anything.

30.3 Rewriting to eliminate offensive references

Review the following sentences for offensive references or terms. If a sentence seems acceptable as written, write C. If a sentence contains unacceptable terms, rewrite it. (See *EasyWriter*, pp. 141–43.) Example:

Passengers
~~Elderly passengers~~ on the cruise ship *Romance Afloat* will enjoy

swimming, shuffleboard, and nightly movies.

1. A West Point cadet must keep his record clean if he expects to excel in his chosen career.

2. All of the children in the kindergarten class will ask their mothers to help make cookies for the bake sale.

3. People like mill workers probably don't listen to the classical music station.

4. Acting as a spokesman and speaking with a southern twang, Cynthia McDowell, attractive mother of two, vowed that all elementary school-teachers in the district would take their turns on the picket line until the school board agreed to resume negotiations.

5. If you can find a mechanic today, see if he will be able to look at the car before morning.

6. Seventy-six-year-old Jewish violinist Josh Mickle, last night's featured soloist, brought the crowd to its feet.

7. Our skylight was installed last week by a woman carpenter.

8. Despite the plane's mechanical problems, the crewmen were able to calm the passengers and land safely.

9. Blind psychology professor Dr. Charles Warnath gave the keynote address last night.

10. Catholic attorney Margaret Samuelson won her sixteenth case in a row last week.

31.1 Considering ethnic and regional varieties of English

Read the following examples by authors using ethnic and regional varieties of English. See if you can "translate" each into standard academic English. Once you have your translated sentences, write a paragraph (in standard academic English) discussing (1) the differences you detect between standard academic English and the ethnic or regional example, and (2) the effects that are achieved by using each variety of English. (See *EasyWriter,* pp. 144–46.)

> "Hey!" squeaked Curtis, his expression amazed. "I got myself shot in the back!"
>
> Beside him, Lyon lifted Curtis' tattered T-shirt, plain and faded black like the other boys' . . . gang colors. "Yeah? Well, you for sure be takin it cool, man. Let's check it out."
>
> . . . Finally, he smiled and parted Curtis' arm. "It be only a cut. Like from a chunk of flyin brick or somethin. Nowhere near his heart. That be all what matter."   —Jess Mowry, *Way Past Cool*

> ". . . You look like you come from here but don't sound it."
>
> "My people came from Quoyle's Point but I was brought up in the States. So I'm an outsider. More or less." Quoyle's hand crept up over his chin.
>
> The harbormaster looked at him. Squinted.
>
> "Yes," said Diddy Shovel. "I guess you got a story there, m'boy. How did it all come about that you was raised so far from home? That you come back?"   —E. Annie Proulx, *The Shipping News*

32.1 Using formal register

Revise each of the following sentences to use formal register consistently, eliminating colloquial or slang terms. (See *EasyWriter,* pp. 146–48.) Example:

> Although be excited   as soon as
> I can ~~get all enthused~~ about writing, ~~but~~ I sit down to write my
> ^   ^ blank.   ^
> mind goes ~~right to sleep.~~
>   ^

1. James Agee's most famous novel, *A Death in the Family*, focuses on a young boy and on what happens after his old man kicks in a car wreck.

2. The young dancers stamped their feet so that their anklets jingled, and the audience eyeballed them approvingly.

3. This essay will trash Mr. Buckley's wacko argument.

4. We decided not to buy a bigger car that got lousy gas mileage and instead to keep our old Honda.

5. Often, instead of firing an incompetent teacher, school officials will transfer the person to another school in order to avoid the hassles involved in a dismissal.

6. After she had raced to the post office at ten minutes to five, she realized that she had completely spaced the fact that it was a federal holiday.

7. Desdemona's attitude is that of a wimp; she just lies down and dies, accepting her death as inevitable.

8. Moby Dick's humongous size was matched only by Ahab's obsessive desire to wipe him out.

9. My family lived in Trinidad for the first ten years of my life, and we went through a lot; but when we came to America, we thought we had it made.

10. The class misbehaved so dreadfully in their regular teacher's absence that the substitute lost it.

32.2 Determining levels of language

For each of the scenarios below, note who the audience would be for the piece of writing. Then circle the level of formality that would be appropriate. Be prepared to explain your answer. (See *EasyWriter*, pp. 146–48.) Example:

An Internet chat room for people who are interested in Harley-Davidson motorcycles

Level of formality:

(informal)　 formal

Audience: _____ *others who share your passion* _____

1. An email to a childhood friend across the country

   Level of formality:

   informal　 formal

   Audience: _____

2. A letter requesting an interview in response to a help-wanted advertisement in the newspaper

   Level of formality:

   informal　 formal

   Audience: _____

3. A brochure explaining the recycling policies of your community to local residents

   Level of formality:

   informal　 formal

   Audience: _____

4. A letter to the editor of the *Washington Post* explaining that a recent editorial failed to consider all the facts about health maintenance organizations (HMOs)

   Level of formality:

   informal　 formal

   Audience: _____

5. A cover letter asking a professor to accept the late paper you are

    sending after the end of the semester.

    Level of formality:

    informal   formal

    Audience: _____

32.3 Checking for correct denotation

Read each of the following sentences, looking for errors in denotation and using your dictionary as needed. Underline every error that you find, determine the word intended, and write in the correct word. If a sentence has no error, write C. (See *EasyWriter*, pp. 148–49.) Example:

> _adapted_
> **Peregrine falcons, once an endangered species, have ~~adopted~~ to**
> ^
> **nesting in cities instead of wilderness areas.**

1. As recently as 1970, many people thought that the distinction of the

    peregrine falcon was inevitable.

2. The falcons' situation reached its apex that year, when there were no

    wild pairs of breeding peregrine falcons anywhere east of the Rocky

    Mountains.

3. Until 1965, the descent of the falcons was blamed on overdevelopment

    and hunting.

4. The real problem, which effected many other large birds, was the

    widespread use of the pesticide DDT.

5. Byproducts of the chemical remain for long periods in the body,

    and the falcons, which are at the top of the food chain, consumed

    concentrated doses.

6. DDT made the shells of the birds' eggs so brittle that they shattered when the falcons tried to incubate them.

7. The federal government banded the use of DDT, but the falcons needed even more assistance from humans.

8. Thin-shelled falcon eggs were taken from nests and replaced by plaster ones so the parent birds had the delusion that they were incubating eggs.

9. Meanwhile, the eggs were hatched in lavatories, and the chicks were returned to their parents' cliffside nests and raised there.

10. Retrofitting the falcons to the East Coast has been wildly successful, and New York City, with its clifflike skyscrapers, is now home to breeding pairs of peregrines.

32.4 Revising sentences to change connotation

The sentences that follow contain words with strongly judgmental connotative meanings. Underline these words; then revise each sentence to make it more neutral. (See *EasyWriter*, pp. 148–49.) Example:

> **The current NRA <u>scheme</u> appeals to patriotism as a <u>smokescreen to obscure the real issue</u> of gun control.**
>
> The current NRA campaign appeals to patriotism rather than responding directly to gun-control proposals.

1. The Democrats are conspiring on a new education bill.

2. CEOs waltz away with millions in salary, stock options, and pensions, whereas the little people who keep the company running get peanuts.

3. Only recently have ladies landed a seat on the Supreme Court.

4. Tree-huggers ranted about the Explorer's gas mileage outside the Ford dealership.

5. Bloodthirsty fans bellowed mindlessly for the referee's head after the call went against the thugs on the home team.

6. Naive voters often stumble to the polls and blithely yank whichever handles are closest to them.

7. Liberals constantly whine about protecting civil rights, but they don't care about protecting the flag that Americans have fought and died for.

8. A mob of protesters appeared, yelling and jabbing their signs in the air.

32.5 Considering connotation

Study the italicized words in each of the following passages, and decide what each word's connotations contribute to your understanding of the passage. Think of a synonym for each word. What difference would the new word make to the effect of the passage? (See *EasyWriter*, pp. 148–49.) Example:

> It is a story of extended horror. But it isn't only the horror that *numbs* response. Nor is it that the discoverer [Columbus] *deteriorates* so steadily after the discovery. It is the *banality* of the man. He was looking less for America or Asia than for gold; and the banality of expectation matches a continuing banality of *perception*.
>
> – V. S. NAIPAUL, "Columbus and Crusoe"
>
> *numbs:* deadens, paralyzes
> *deteriorates:* declines, gets worse
> *banality:* ordinariness, triviality
> *perception:* understanding, judgment

1. The Burmans were already *racing* past me across the mud. It was obvious that the elephant would never *rise* again, but he was not dead. He was breathing very rhythmically with long *rattling* gasps, his great *mound* of a side painfully rising and falling.

    – GEORGE ORWELL, "Shooting an Elephant"

2. Then one evening Miss Glory told me to serve the ladies on the porch. After I set the tray down and turned toward the kitchen, one of the

women asked, "What's your name, *girl*?"

– MAYA ANGELOU, I Know Why the Caged Bird Sings

3. We caught two bass, *hauling* them in *briskly* as though they were mackerel, pulling them over the side of the boat in a *businesslike* manner without any landing net, and stunning them with a *blow* on the back of the head.

– E. B. WHITE, "Once More to the Lake"

4. The Kiowas are a summer people; they *abide* the cold and keep to themselves; but when the season *turns* and the land becomes warm and *vital*, they cannot *hold still*.

– N. SCOTT MOMADAY, "The Way to Rainy Mountain"

5. If boxing is a sport, it is the most *tragic* of all sports because, more than any [other] human activity, it *consumes* the very excellence it *displays:* Its very *drama* is this consumption.   – JOYCE CAROL OATES, "On Boxing"

32.6 Using specific and concrete words

Rewrite each of the following sentences to be more specific and more concrete. (See *EasyWriter*, p. 149.) Example:

The weather this summer has varied.

July and August have offered two extremes of weather, going from clear, dry days, on which the breeze seems to scrub the sky, to the dog days of oppressive humidity.

1. The child played on the beach.

2. He isn't terribly handsome, but he's a lot of fun.

3. The attendant came toward my car.

4. Children sometimes behave badly in public.

5. The entryway of the building was dirty.

6. Robert was not feeling well, so he stayed home from the party.

7. My neighbor is a nuisance.

8. Sunday dinner was good.

9. The sounds at dawn are memorable.

10. Central Texas has an unusual climate.

32.7 Thinking about similes and metaphors

Identify the similes and metaphors in the following numbered items, and decide how each contributes to your understanding of the passage or sentence in which it appears. (See *EasyWriter*, pp. 149–50.) Example:

> **The tattoo he had gotten as a teenager, now a blue bruise underneath the word "Mom," remained his favorite souvenir.**

a blue bruise (metaphor): makes vivid the tattoo's appearance

1. The fog hangs among the trees like veils of trailing lace.
   — STEPHANIE VAUGHN, "My Mother Breathing Light"

2. The clouds were great mounds of marshmallow fluff heaped just below the wings of the passing airplane.

3. The migraine acted as a circuit breaker, and the fuses have emerged intact.
   — JOAN DIDION, "In Bed"

4. As Serena began to cry, James felt as if someone had punched him in the stomach.

5. Black women are called, in the folklore that so aptly identifies one's status in society, "the mule of the world," because we have been handed the burdens that everyone else—everyone else—refused to carry.
   — ALICE WALKER, *In Search of Our Mothers' Gardens*

6. John's mother, Mom Willie, who wore her Southern background like a magnolia corsage, eternally fresh, was robust and in her sixties.
   – MAYA ANGELOU, "The Heart of a Woman"

7. According to Dr. Seuss, the Grinch is a bad banana with a greasy black peel.

8. I was watching everyone else and didn't see the waitress standing quietly by. Her voice was deep and soft like water moving in a cavern.
   – WILLIAM LEAST HEAT MOON, "In the Land of 'Coke-Cola'"

9. The clicking sounds of the rotary phone were as old-fashioned and charming as the song of a square dance caller.

10. My horse, when he is in his stall or lounging about the pasture, has the same relationship to pain that I have when cuddling up with a good murder mystery — comfort and convenience have top priority.
    – VICKI HEARNE, "Horses in Partnership with Time"

Multilingual Writers

34.1 Identifying count and noncount nouns

Identify each of the common nouns in the following short paragraph as either a count or a noncount noun. (See *EasyWriter*, pp. 154–55.) The first one has been done for you.

        count
    In his <u>book</u> *Hiroshima*, John Hersey tells the story of six people who survived the destruction of Hiroshima on August 6, 1945. The bomb detonated at 8:15 in the morning. When the explosion occurred, Mrs. Hatsuyo Nakamura was looking out her window and watching a neighbor at work on his house. The force of the explosion lifted her into the air and carried her into the next room, where she was buried by roofing tiles and other debris. When she crawled out, she heard her daughter, Myeko, calling out; she was buried up to her waist and could not move.

34.2 Using appropriate noun phrases

Each of the following sentences contains an error with a noun phrase. Revise each sentence. (See *EasyWriter*, pp. 155–56.) Example:

               a
Many people use small sponge to clean their kitchen counters.
                 ^

1. Bacteria are invisible organisms that can sometimes make the people sick.

2. Dangerous germs such as salmonella are commonly found in a some foods.

3. When a cook prepares chicken on cutting board, salmonella germs may be left on the board.

4. Much people regularly clean their kitchen counters and cutting boards to remove bacteria.

5. Unfortunately, a warm, wet kitchen sponge is a ideal home for bacteria.

6. Every time someone wipes a counter with dirty sponge, more germ are spread around the kitchen.

7. Microwaving a dirty sponge for one minute will kill a most bacteria that live in it.

8. According to research studies, the young single men's kitchens tend to have a fewer germs than other kitchen.

9. These surprising fact tells researchers that young single men do not often wipe their kitchen counters.

34.3 Using articles appropriately

Insert articles as necessary in the following passage. If no article is needed, leave the space blank. (See *EasyWriter*, pp. 155–56.) Example:

One of _____the_____ **things that makes** _____ **English unique**

is _____the_____ **number of** _____ **English words.**

_____ English language has _____ very large vocabulary.
About _____ 200,000 words are in _____ everyday use, and if
_____ less common words are included, _____ total reaches
more than _____ million. This makes _____ English
_____ rich language, but also _____ difficult one to learn well.
In addition, _____ rules of English grammar are sometimes confus-
ing. They were modeled on _____ Latin rules, even though _____
two languages are very different. Finally, _____ fact that _____
English has _____ large number of _____ words imported

from _____ other languages makes _____ English spelling

very hard to master. _____ English is now _____ most widely

used language around _____ world, so _____ educated people

are expected to know it.

35.1 Identifying verbs and verb phrases

Underline each verb or verb phrase in the following sentences. (See *EasyWriter*, pp. 156–59.) Example:

> **Many cultures <u>celebrate</u> the arrival of spring with a festival of some kind.**

1. The spring festival of Holi occurs in northern India every March during the full moon.

2. Holi is known as the festival of colors, not only because spring brings flowers, but also because Holi celebrations always include brightly colored dyes.

3. According to legend, the festival of colors began thousands of years ago when Krishna played pranks on girls in his village and threw water on them.

4. During Holi, people toss fistfuls of powdered dyes or dye-filled water balloons at each other and sing traditional Holi songs.

5. Holi festivals allow people freedoms that would be unthinkable during the rest of the year.

6. Any person who is walking outside during a Holi celebration will soon be wearing colored powders or colored water.

7. Men, women, and children can throw powders or dye-filled balloons at anyone, even if the person is much older or of much higher status than they are.

8. Many people wear white clothing for Holi.

9. By the end of the celebration, the white clothes are a riot of color.

10. Doesn't Holi sound like fun?

35.2 Using the present, present perfect, and past forms of verbs

Rewrite the following passage by adding appropriate forms of *have* and main-verb endings or forms for the verbs in parentheses. (See *EasyWriter*, pp. 157–59.) Example:

I _____like_____ **(like) to try new foods, so I ____have eaten____**

(eat) in many different kinds of restaurants in my life.

Several times, I _____ (hear) people musing about the

bravery of the first person who ever _____ (eat) a lobster. It

_____ (be) an interesting question: What do you

_____ (think) _____ (make) anyone do such a

thing? But personally, I _____ (wonder) all my life about how

ancient people _____ (discover) the art of baking bread. After

all, preparing a lobster _____ (be) pretty simple in comparison

to baking. Bread _____ (feed) vast numbers of people for

centuries, so it certainly _____ (be) a more important food

source than lobster, too. Those of us who _____ (love) either

lobster or bread (or both) _____ (be) grateful to those who

_____ (give) us such a wonderful culinary legacy.

35.3 Using specified forms of verbs

Using the subjects and verbs provided, write the specified sentences. (See *EasyWriter*, pp. 157–59.) Example:

> **subject: *Bernie* verb: *touch***
> **sentence using a present form:** Bernie touches the soft fur.
> **sentence using the auxiliary verb *had*:** Bernie had touched a squid before.

1. subject: *they* verb: *decide*

   sentence using a present form:

   sentence using an auxiliary verb + the past participle form:

2. subject: *someone* verb: *follow*

   sentence using a past form:

   sentence using an auxiliary verb + the present participle form:

3. subject: *we* verb: *ask*

   sentence using a present form:

   sentence using the auxiliary *had* + the past participle form:

4. subject: *geese* verb: *migrate*

   sentence using a past form:

   sentence using an auxiliary verb + the present participle form:

5. subject: *baby* verb: *sleep*

   sentence using a present form:

   sentence using an auxiliary verb + past participle form:

6. subject: *teenagers* verb: *consume*

   sentence using a past form:

   sentence using the auxiliary verb *were* + the present participle form:

7. subject: *judge* verb: *expect*

   sentence using a present form:

   sentence using an auxiliary verb + a present participle form:

8. subject: *pasta* verb: *steam*

   sentence using a past form:

   sentence using an auxiliary verb + present participle form:

9. subject: *pilots* verb: *fly*

   sentence using a past form:

   sentence using an auxiliary verb + a present participle form:

10. subject: *hamburger* verb: *taste*

    sentence using a present form:

    sentence using an auxiliary verb + a past participle form:

35.4 Identifying tenses and forms of verbs

From the following list, identify the form of each verb or verb phrase in each of the numbered sentences. (See *EasyWriter*, pp. 157–59.)

simple present	past perfect
simple past	present progressive
present perfect	past progressive

Example:

> **Judge Cohen considered the two arguments.** Simple past

1. On the right side of the room, Monica is demonstrating the Heimlich maneuver.

2. Your children were talking throughout the entire movie.

3. She exercises to reduce stress.

4. As guests were arriving, Cheryl was still getting dressed.

5. Just as we took our seats, the movie began.

6. I have attempted that math problem several times now.

7. Paul required special medical attention for years.

8. My mother has driven the same Mazda for ten years.

9. Horror movies rarely make much of an impression on me, but this one has made me afraid to go out into the parking lot.

10. She had forgotten the assignment.

35.5   Using verbs appropriately

Each of the following sentences contains an error with verbs. Revise each sentence. (See *EasyWriter*, pp. 157–59.) Example:

<blockquote>
    could not
Linguists ~~cannot~~ **interpret hieroglyphics before they discovered the**
      ^
Rosetta Stone.
</blockquote>

1. A French engineer was finding a stone half-buried in the mud by the Nile River in Egypt in 1799.

2. The Rosetta Stone is cover with inscriptions in three ancient languages.

3. The inscription at the top of the stone written in Egyptian hieroglyphics, or pictographs, while the lower part gives the same information in an ancient Egyptian language called Demotic and in ancient Greek.

4. At that time, scholars were puzzled by hieroglyphics for centuries.

5. Very soon after its discovery, the French have made copies of the stone.

6. A scholar named Jean François Champollion could understood both ancient Greek and modern Egyptian, known as Coptic.

7. Champollion knew that he can figure out the Demotic script based on his knowledge of Coptic.

8. From the Demotic inscription, he has learned to read the hieroglyphics.

9. The story of the Rosetta Stone is probably more fascinated than the contents of its inscription.

10. The hieroglyphics and the Demotic and Greek texts all are containing a decree from an ancient king.

35.6 Using infinitives and gerunds appropriately

Revise the following sentences as necessary so that each contains an appropriate infinitive or gerund positioned well. If a sentence does not contain an error, write C. (See *EasyWriter,* pp. 159–60.) Example:

> that
> **It pleases me ^you like me.**

1. We discussed to go to a movie, but we could not agree on what to see.

2. Ashok refused answering his sister's questions.

3. Her mother stopped to drive on her ninetieth birthday.

4. What he has to say is of great interest to me.

5. No one expected being allowed to leave work before midnight.

6. We appreciated to get the invitation.

35.7 Writing conditional sentences

Revise each of the following sentences so that both the *if* clause and the main, or independent, clause contain appropriate verb forms. If a sentence does not contain an error, write C. (See *EasyWriter,* pp. 160–61.) Example:

> **If you want to work as a computer programmer, you ~~would~~**
> are
> **probably ~~be~~ having a hard time finding a high-paying U.S. job**
> ^
> **these days.**

1. Until recently, many people thought that U.S. computer jobs will go unfilled unless college-educated foreign workers will be allowed to work in this country.

2. If the dot-com boom had continued, that prediction might come true.

3. Instead, many highly skilled U.S. technology workers will have few options if they became unemployed tomorrow.

4. If any computer job is announced these days, hundreds of qualified people applied for it.

5. Today, if a company uses many programmers or other computer experts, it may hire workers in India to fill the positions.

6. If Indian workers would require as much money as Americans do to live, U.S. companies would not be as eager to outsource computer work to the other side of the world.

7. If business owners cared more about keeping good jobs at home, they hired skilled workers here instead of skilled workers in another country.

8. Will fewer Americans be unemployed right now if the dot-com boom had never happened?

9. Some young people in this country would not have gotten useless technology degrees if they knew how the economy would decline.

10. If American students would want to prepare for a secure future, they should consider a specialty such as nursing, in which jobs are available and the work cannot be sent abroad.

36.1 Using prepositions idiomatically

Insert one or more appropriate prepositions in each of the following sentences. (See *EasyWriter*, pp. 162–63.) Example:

We will have the answer ____by____ four o'clock this afternoon.

1. Children should have pencils _____ their pencil cases.

2. How can schools help when children arrive _____ the morning without breakfast?

3. Education requires participation _____ all of us.

4. Children should fall _____ love with reading.

5. Adults who read to children can provide good examples _____ them.

6. Students should get to school precisely _____ time.

7. Having someone to help them _____ home gives struggling students more confidence.

8. Schools themselves may be struggling _____ financial cutbacks and poor facilities.

9. Classrooms need books _____ their shelves.

10. A high-quality public education should be given _____ every child.

36.2 Recognizing and using two-word verbs

Identify each italicized expression as either a two-word verb or a verb + preposition. (See *EasyWriter,* p. 164.) Example:

Look up John Brown the next time you're in town.   two-word verb

1. George was still *looking for* his keys when we left.

2. I always *turn down* the thermostat when I go to bed or leave the house.

3. We drank a pitcher of lemonade in an attempt to *cool* ourselves *off* on a sweltering July afternoon.

4. Marion *gave back* the ring she had gotten as an engagement gift.

5. Jimmy *takes after* his father, poor thing.

6. The car *turned into* the driveway.

7. The frog *turned into* a prince.

8. The camp counselor *handed* the candy *out* as if it were gold.

9. *Put* the garbage *out* on the sidewalk, please.

10. Don't *put* yourself *out* on my behalf.

37.1 Expressing subjects and objects explicitly

Revise the following sentences or nonsentences as necessary so that they have explicit subjects and objects. If a sentence does not contain an error, write C. (See *EasyWriter*, pp. 165–66.) Example:

> It is
> ~~Is~~ easy and convenient for people with access to computers to shop
> online.

1. No faster way to take care of holiday shopping.

2. Computers also allow people to buy items they cannot find locally.

3. Banks and credit-card companies have Web sites now, and consumers use for making payments, looking at statements, and transferring balances.

4. Are problems with doing everything online, of course.

5. Customers must use credit cards, and thieves want to break in and get.

6. Are small-time thieves and pranksters disrupting online services.

7. Jamming popular sites is one way for hackers to gain notoriety, and have been several examples of this action.

8. A hacker can get enormous amounts of online data, even if is supposed to be secure.

9. People should be concerned about online privacy because is a tremendous amount of private information stored in online database.

10. Internet users must use caution and common sense online, but is also essential for online information to be safeguarded by security experts.

37.2   Editing for English word order

Revise the following sentences as necessary. If a sentence does not
contain an error, write C. (See *EasyWriter*, p. 166.) Example:

1. To sleep he wishes to go now.

2. He displays proudly in the window a flag.

3. Comes in first the runner from Kenya.

4. She should go not into the woods alone.

5. A passing grade she wants.

6. Extremely poorly Sandy drove during her first road test.

7. The road winds lazily through the fields.

8. Desserts some restaurant guests would like to begin with.

9. John watches videos incessantly.

10. "Speak fluently English," ordered the instructor.

Answers to the Even-Numbered Exercises

FIND IT. FIX IT.

Recognizing and eliminating the twenty most common errors

Some sentences have errors that most people would correct in the same way; some sentences contain errors that have various solutions. Students may wish to make changes in addition to the corrections noted.

2. Today, we often forget how dangerous childhood diseases can be. Less than a century ago, many children did not survive to adulthood because of diphtheria, whooping cough, and measles. Fortunately, such ailments are rare nowadays; however, if people decide not to immunize their children, these illnesses could easily make a comeback.

4. [The first sentence is missing commas.] I was gaining speed and feeling really good, but when I looked back, he wasn't there.

6. [The error is in the second sentence.] After all, it is they who will support us with things like money, food, and clothes until we are capable of living on our own.

8. [The errors are in the third sentence.] And if you get extremely lost, pulling off and asking is the easiest way to get on track.

10. [The errors are in both sentences.] Nancy told Lois that Lois needed to work overtime on Friday. This demand violated company rules.

12. [The error is in the second sentence.] He even named his new puppy Einstein, but that didn't prevent the dog from chasing its tail.

14. [The error is in the second sentence.] Those university representatives who argue that students and professors should rely on an honor system believe that investigating student essays does more harm than good.

16. [The error is in the second sentence.] Children in extremely unhappy homes will not necessarily be more miserable if their parents divorce.

18. [The error is in the first sentence.] In the attic, we found several old board games that no one remembered how to play.

20. [The error is in the first sentence.] The knights, with armor and horses beautifully decorated, participate in battles of jousting, target shooting with spears, archery, and duels of strategy and strength using swords and shields.

WRITING

EXERCISE 2.2 Recognizing arguable statements

2. factual

4. factual

6. arguable

8. factual

10. arguable

SENTENCE GRAMMAR

EXERCISE 7.1 Identifying verbs

2. favored

4. called; outlawed

6. was developed

8. has given

10. were

EXERCISE 7.2 Using irregular verb forms

2. was; said; was

4. broke; lay

6. met; fell

8. kept; was

10. grown; spread

EXERCISE 7.3 Editing verb forms

2. freezed—froze

4. ate—eaten

6. C

8. knowed—known

10. C

EXERCISE 7.4 Distinguishing between *lie* and *lay, sit* and *set, rise* and *raise*

2. raise

4. rose

6. set

8. rose

10. lies

EXERCISE 7.5 Deciding on verb tenses

2. invited

4. was

6. interrogated; died

8. showed / had shown

10. began; became

EXERCISE 7.6 Sequencing tenses

2. Until I *started* knitting again last month, I *had forgotten* how.

4. After Darius said that he wanted to postpone college, I *tried* to talk him out of it.

6. They *had hoped* to plant their garden by now.

8. C

10. *Having cut off* all contact with family, he *had* no one to ask for help.

EXERCISE 7.7 Converting the voice of a sentence

Answers may vary slightly.

2. The storm *uprooted* huge pine trees.

4. Jerry *ate* the last doughnut in the box just a few minutes ago.

6. For months, the mother kangaroo *protects, feeds,* and *teaches* its baby how to survive.

8. The first snow of winter *covered* the lawns and rooftops.

10. Suddenly, the roof over our heads *was being pounded on* by rainfall.

EXERCISE 7.8 Using subjunctive mood

2. C
4. would have heard—had heard
6. knows—know
8. should not take—not take
10. was—were

EXERCISE 8.1 Selecting verbs that agree with their subjects

2. are
4. include
6. offer
8. looks
10. does

EXERCISE 8.2 Making subjects and verbs agree

2. are—is
4. use—uses
6. sets—set
8. C
10. allows—allow
12. C
14. belongs—belong

EXERCISE 9.1 Identifying adjectives and adverbs

Adjectives are set in *italics;* adverbs are set in **boldface**.

2. **agonizingly; slowly; finally**
4. *The;* **somewhat;** *shy;* **reluctantly;** *six; exuberant*
6. *The; youngest; the; a; brilliant*
8. **Never; before;** *one; a; bigger; this*
10. *Imminent; many;* **constantly**

EXERCISE 9.2 Adding adjectives and adverbs

SUGGESTED ANSWERS

2.   Surely, most of us enjoy classic movies.

4.   A multinational corporation can fire undependable workers.

6.   The unpopulated boardwalk crosses the bleak, wintry beach.

8.   The mainstream media are determinedly ignoring his candidacy.

10.   Which way did you say the hunted pair went yesterday?

EXERCISE 9.3 Using adjectives and adverbs appropriately

2.   defiant—defiantly; modifies *crosses*

4.   sadly—sad; modifies *you*

6.   relievedly—relieved; modifies *you*

8.   oddly—odd; modifies *"words"*

10.   Lucky—Luckily; modifies *available*

EXERCISE 9.4 Using comparative and superlative modifiers appropriately

SUGGESTED ANSWERS

2.   to live longer—to live longer than men

4.   the largest—the larger

6.   the famousest—the most famous

8.   unpleasantest—most unpleasant

10.   the most unique—a unique

EXERCISE 10.1 Revising sentences with misplaced modifiers

SUGGESTED ANSWERS

2.   The tenor, singing with verve, captivated the entire audience.

4.   The city spent approximately twelve million dollars on the new stadium.

6.   On the day in question, the patient was not able to breathe normally.

8.   The clothes that I was giving away were full of holes.

10.   A wailing baby with a soggy diaper was quickly kissed by the candidate.

EXERCISE 10.2 Revising squinting modifiers, disruptive modifiers, and split infinitives

SUGGESTED ANSWERS

2. He vividly remembered enjoying the sound of Mrs. McIntosh's singing.

4. The mayor promised that she would not raise taxes after her reelection.

   After her reelection, the mayor promised that she would not raise taxes.

6. The collector who originally owned the painting planned to leave it to a museum.

   The collector who owned the painting planned originally to leave it to a museum.

8. Doctors can now restore limbs that have been partially severed to a functioning condition.

   Doctors can now restore limbs that have been severed to a partially functioning condition.

10. The speaker said he would answer questions when he finished.

    When he finished, the speaker said he would answer questions.

12. After a long summer under the blazing sun, the compost smelled pretty bad when I turned it.

14. After a long day at work and an evening class, Stella did not want to argue about who was going to do the dishes.

    Stella did not want to argue about who was going to do the dishes after a long day at work and an evening class.

EXERCISE 10.3 Revising dangling modifiers

SUGGESTED ANSWERS

2. When interviewing grieving relatives, reporters show no consideration for their privacy.

4. Newscasters, who may be chosen for their looks, often have weak journalistic credentials.

6. Assuming that viewers care about no one except Americans, editorial boards for network news shows reject many international stories.

8. Horrified by stories of bloodshed, most viewers don't recognize the low probability of becoming a victim of crime or terrorism.

10. Because news broadcasts do not cover less sensational but more common dangers such as reckless driving and diabetes, they do not tell viewers what is really likely to hurt them.

12. Journalists reporting on a national story may focus on speculation about causes instead of on what actually happened.

14. Whether political discussions are on talk radio or on political talk shows on television, distortions and bias are the norm.

EXERCISE 11.1 Identifying pronouns and antecedents

Pronouns are set in *italics;* antecedents are set in **boldface**.

2. **dogs;** *that; their*

4. *they; their;* **volunteers; puppy;** *its*

6. *you;* **puppy;** *its;* **coat;** *that; it*

8. *Some;* **pups;** *these*

10. *you; your*

EXERCISE 11.2 Using subjective-case pronouns

2. they

4. they

6. they

8. We

10. she

EXERCISE 11.3 Using objective-case pronouns

2. C

4. When we asked, the seller promised us that the software would work on a Macintosh computer.

6. Max told Jackson and him that the cabin was available to them.

8. C

10. We need two volunteers: you and Tom.

EXERCISE 11.4 Using possessive-case pronouns

2. mine

4. Her

6. their

8. her

10. yours

EXERCISE 11.5 Using *who, whoever, whom,* or *whomever*

2. Whoever

4. whoever

6. Whom

8. whom

10. whoever

EXERCISE 11.6 Using pronouns in compound structures, appositives, elliptical clauses; choosing between *we* and *us* before a noun

2. he

4. he

6. her

8. them

10. he

12. us

14. I

EXERCISE 11.7 Maintaining pronoun–antecedent agreement

SUGGESTED ANSWERS

2. A child-free person may feel that people with children see his or her time as less valuable than their own.

4. Child-free employees may feel that they have to subsidize family medical plans at work for people who have children.

6. However, a community has to consider the welfare of its children because caring for and educating children eventually benefits everyone.

8. Almost no one would be able to afford to have children if parents were expected to pay for educating and training their offspring entirely without help.

10. As writer Barbara Kingsolver once pointed out, even people without children will probably need the services of a doctor or a mechanic in their old age.

EXERCISE 11.8 Clarifying pronoun reference

SUGGESTED ANSWERS

2. Not long after the company set up the subsidiary, the subsidiary went bankrupt.

Not long after the company set up the subsidiary, the company went bankrupt.

4. When Deyon was reunited with his father, the boy wept.

   When Deyon was reunited with his father, his father wept.

6. The weather forecast said to expect snow in the overnight hours.

8. Lear divides his kingdom between the two older daughters, Goneril and Regan, whose extravagant professions of love are more flattering than the simple affection of the youngest daughter, Cordelia. The consequences of this error in judgment soon become apparent, as the older daughters prove neither grateful nor kind to him.

10. The visit to the pyramids was canceled because of the recent terrorist attacks on tourists there, so Kay, who had waited years to see the monuments, was disappointed.

EXERCISE 12.1 Revising comma splices and fused sentences

Only one suggested answer is given for each numbered item.

2. The group Human Rights Watch filed a report on Mauritania, a nation in northwest Africa.

4. Members of Mauritania's ruling group are called the Beydanes, an Arab Berber tribe also known as the White Moors.

6. In modern-day Mauritania, many of the Haratin are still slaves; they serve the Beydanes.

8. Mauritania outlawed slavery in 1981, but little has been done to enforce the law.

10. Physical force is not usually used to enslave the Haratin. Rather, they are held by the force of conditioning.

12. By some estimates 300,000 former slaves, who are psychologically and economically dependent, still serve their old masters.

14. In addition, there may be as many as 90,000 Haratin still enslaved; some Beydanes have refused to free their slaves unless the government pays compensation.

16. Of course, slavery must have existed in Mauritania, or there would have been no compelling reason to make a decree to abolish it in 1981.

18. Both the slaveholding Beydanes and the enslaved Haratin are made up largely of Muslims, so some people in Mauritania see resistance to slavery in their country as anti-Muslim.

20. Islamic authorities in Mauritania have agreed that all Muslims are equal; therefore, one Muslim must not enslave another.

EXERCISE 13.1 Eliminating sentence fragments

SUGGESTED ANSWERS

2. Her father pulled strings to get her the job. Later he regretted his actions.

4. I must have looked ridiculous trying to carry a portfolio, art box, illustration boards, and drawing pads.

6. Connie picked up the cat and started playing with it. It scratched her neck with its sharp little claws.

8. The region has dry, sandy soil, blown into strange formations by the ever-present wind.

10. Many older Americans want nothing more than to feel useful.

SENTENCE STYLE

EXERCISE 14.1 Matching subjects and predicates

SUGGESTED ANSWERS

2. Many of her books deal with the aftermath of slavery and often feature strong women characters.

   Her books, many of which deal with the aftermath of slavery, often feature strong women characters.

4. Although Morrison's depictions of African American families and neighborhoods are realistic, they also include supernatural elements.

   Morrison's depictions of African American families and neighborhoods are realistic, but they also include supernatural elements.

6. *Song of Solomon* was hailed as a masterpiece, winning the National Book Critics Circle Award in 1978.

   Song of Solomon, hailed as a masterpiece, won the National Book Critics Circle Award in 1978.

8. The title character in *Beloved* is the ghost of a murdered infant inhabiting the body of a young woman.

   Beloved features the ghost of a murdered infant inhabiting the body of a young woman.

10. In 1993, Toni Morrison became the first African American woman to be awarded the Nobel Prize in literature.

Toni Morrison, who was awarded the Nobel Prize in literature in 1993, was the first African American woman to win that prize.

EXERCISE 14.2 Making comparisons complete, consistent, and clear

SUGGESTED ANSWERS

2. New York City has a more diverse culture than any other metropolis in the United States.

4. As time went on, the baby became less animated and less interested.

6. The car's exterior is blue, but the seats are black vinyl.

8. Are citizens of the United States now as safe as or safer than they were before September 11, 2001?

10. She argued that children are even more important for men than they are for women.

EXERCISE 15.1 Identifying conjunctions

2. for

4. When

6. until

EXERCISE 15.3 Writing sentences with subordination

SUGGESTED ANSWERS

2. At my parents' house, I spent a long night on a sleep sofa that has an uncomfortably thin mattress with a hard metal bar beneath it.

4. Walking into the shelter, I saw men, women, and children slumped against the wall, their belongings lying in overturned shopping carts.

EXERCISE 16.1 Eliminating unnecessary words and phrases

SUGGESTED ANSWERS

2. Shortly after Houdini's birth, his family moved to Appleton, where his father served as the only rabbi.

4. His many escapes included getting out of a giant sealed envelope without tearing it and walking out of jail cells that were said to be escape-proof.

6. Clearly, Houdini did not want anyone to know his secrets.

8. Houdini's tremendous control over almost every muscle allowed him to contort his body into seemingly impossible positions.

10. On his deathbed, Houdini promised his wife that he would try to make contact with her from beyond the grave, but so far, he has not been able to get in touch.

EXERCISE 17.1 Creating parallel words or phrases

SUGGESTED ANSWERS

2. I want not only hot fudge but also whipped cream.

4. I told my younger sister to keep out of my clothes and to keep away from my friends.

6. When he got his promotion, he told the neighbors, called his family, and took out an ad in the newspaper.

8. We must either walk quickly or drive slowly.

10. The contract required the workers to come in late at night and to keep quiet about what they saw.

EXERCISE 17.2 Revising sentences for parallelism

SUGGESTED ANSWERS

2. Many people in this country remember dancing to the mambo music of the 1950s and listening to that era's Latin bands.

4. Growing up near Havana and studying classical piano, Pérez Prado loved Cuban music.

6. Playing piano in Havana nightclubs, arranging music for a Latin big band, and joining jam sessions with the band's guitarists gave him the idea for a new kind of music.

8. Prado conducted his orchestra by waving his hands, moving his head and shoulders, and kicking his feet high in the air.

10. Pérez Prado, an innovator and a great musician, died in 1989.

EXERCISE 18.1 Revising for verb tense and mood

SUGGESTED ANSWERS

2. C

4. All health care workers should know that they have to keep their hands clean.

6. Hand-washing can be repetitive, time consuming, and boring, but it is crucial to patient safety in every hospital.

8. The bacteria that cause these infections cannot travel through the air. They require physical contact to move from place to place.

10. Wash your hands frequently, and follow these instructions even if your skin gets dry.

EXERCISE 18.2 Eliminating shifts in voice and point of view

Suggested answers

2. I liked the sense of individualism, the crowd yelling for me, and the feeling that I was in command.

4. When someone says "roommate" to a high school senior bound for college, that senior conjures up thoughts of no privacy and potential fights.

6. We knew that we shouldn't walk across the railroad trestle, but we went ahead anyway.

8. Lionel gathered the roses and then arranged them.

10. Suddenly we heard an explosion of wings off to our right, and we could see a hundred or more ducks lifting off from the water.

EXERCISE 18.3 Eliminating shifts between direct and indirect discourse

Suggested answers

2. She said that during a semester abroad she really missed all her friends.

4. Loren Eiseley feels an urge to join the birds in their soundless flight, but in the end he understands that he cannot because he is "only a man."

EXERCISE 18.4 Eliminating shifts in tone and diction

Suggested answers

2. The Chinese invented noodles, though many people believe the Italians created them.

4. The Guggenheim exhibit of African works of art, often misunderstood and undervalued by Western art historians, is a mind-expanding show.

PUNCTUATION/MECHANICS

EXERCISE 19.1 Using a comma to set off introductory elements

2. In the past,

4. Of course,

6. Someday,

8. Naturally,

10. Unable to judge whether smells are delectable or nauseating,

EXERCISE 19.2 Using a comma in compound sentences

SUGGESTED ANSWERS

2. Over two decades ago, fertility treatments were a little-explored field, so the first "test-tube baby" astonished the world.

4. A scientist combines an egg cell and a sperm cell, and an embryo forms when the egg cell begins to divide.

6. The procedure requires scientific intervention, yet the parents of a "test-tube baby" have a child that is biologically theirs.

8. In vitro fertilization has helped many people have children, but it is expensive.

10. The first "test-tube baby," who was born in England, was a celebrity, but today, children whose parents used in vitro fertilization are quite common.

EXERCISE 19.3 Recognizing restrictive and nonrestrictive elements

2. The clause *that preserves a cadaver* is essential for the sentence to have meaning. Therefore, it should not take commas.

4. The appositive phrase *reading Web logs* is not needed to make the meaning of the sentence clear. It should be set off with commas.

6. The appositive phrase *the first African American to serve on the U.S. Supreme Court* provides nonessential information. Therefore, the phrase requires commas to set it off.

8. The clause *who created South Park* does not contain essential information, so it should be set off with commas.

10. The clause *which had spared Waterville* is nonrestrictive because it provides additional, not essential, information. Therefore, it requires commas to set it off.

EXERCISE 19.4 Using commas to set off items in a series

2. I am looking forward to turning eighteen, being able to vote, and perhaps serving in the military.

4. The moon circles the earth, the earth revolves around the sun, and the sun is just one star among many in the Milky Way galaxy.

6. C

8. The firm's quiet, pleasant, excessively polite public relations executives made everyone a little nervous.

10. Superficial observation does not provide accurate insight into people's lives—how they feel, what they believe in, how they respond to others.

EXERCISE 19.5 Using commas to set off parenthetical and transitional expressions, contrasting elements, interjections, direct address, and tag questions

2. Madame President, I move to adjourn the meeting.

4. The West, in fact, has become solidly Republican in presidential elections.

6. Captain Kirk, I'm a doctor, not a madman.

8. One must consider the society as a whole, not just its parts.

10. Mary announced, "Kids, I want you to clean your rooms, not make a bigger mess."

EXERCISE 19.6 Using commas with dates, addresses, and quotations

2. C

4. "Who can match the desperate humorlessness of the adolescent who thinks he is the first to discover seriousness?" asks P. J. Kavanaugh.

6. The ship was hit by two torpedoes on May 7, 1915, and sank in minutes.

EXERCISE 19.7 Eliminating unnecessary and inappropriate commas

2. Insomniacs do indeed wake up at night, but studies have demonstrated that they also have trouble napping during the day.

4. In many cases, insomniacs suffer from anxiety.

6. C

8. Sleep therapists recommend going to bed at the same time every night, not watching television in bed, and not reading in bed.

10. Although tired people are more dangerous drivers and less productive workers, no one knows for certain if insomnia can actually make them sick.

EXERCISE 20.1 Using semicolons to link clauses

2. Teenagers today don't spend all their time on the telephone; instead, they go online and send each other instant messages.

4. The unwanted package arrived C.O.D.; I politely refused to pay the charges.

6. Pittsburgh was once notorious for its smoke and grime; today, its skies and streets are cleaner than those of many other American cities.

8. Establishing your position in an office is an important task; your profile will mold your relationships with other staff members.

10. Florida's mild winter climate is ideal for bicycling; in addition, the terrain is very flat.

EXERCISE 20.2 Eliminating misused semicolons

2. Verbal scores have decreased by more than fifty-four points, while math scores have decreased by more than thirty-six.

4. Finally, I found her at the Humane Society: a beautiful shepherd-collie mix who likes children and plays well with cats.

6. He left a large estate, which was used to endow a scholarship fund.

8. You can't take your ball and go home just because you think you'll lose the game.

10. The speech made sense to some observers, but not to me.

EXERCISE 21.1 Using periods appropriately

2. She has raised disturbing questions about why parents sometimes kill their offspring.

4. Human parents, even in recent centuries, may actively or passively have limited their children's chances to grow up.

6. The term "parent-offspring conflict" was coined by Robert Trivers, PhD.

8. Many mothers are indeed willing to put up with a great deal from their children, from 2:00 a.m. feedings through requests for college tuition.

10. Describing a mother's crime against her child as "inhuman" is neither accurate nor helpful in preventing future tragedies.

EXERCISE 21.2 Using question marks appropriately

2. "Can I play this?" asked Manuel.

4. "How long are we supposed to wait for Sara?" wondered Erin.

6. C

8. C

EXERCISE 21.3 Using exclamation points appropriately

SUGGESTED ANSWERS

2. Oh, no! We've lost the house!

4. "Go! Go! Go!" roared the crowd as the quarterback sped toward the end zone.

EXERCISE 22.1 Using apostrophes to signal possession

2. Recipients who pass on messages want everyone to hear about a *child's* inspiring fight against cancer or about some dangerous drug, product, or disease.

4. A *hoax's* creators count on *recipients'* kind hearts and concern for the well-being of their families and friends.

6. Have you heard the one about how a *deodorant's* ingredients supposedly clog your pores and cause cancer?

8. Some of these scares are probably intended to damage certain *corporations'* reputations by spreading rumors about products.

10. The *Internet's* speed has allowed such anonymous rumors to spread more rapidly than anyone would have thought possible twenty years ago.

EXERCISE 22.2 Using apostrophes appropriately

2. I can't believe you haven't started the paper yet; it's due tomorrow morning.

4. That guy who's been giving you a ride after work called at about nine o'clock.

6. The clothes that I'm washing now didn't really get too dirty.

8. The distributor says that your order has not received its approval from the business office.

10. That cat of yours is nothing but trouble.

EXERCISE 23.1 Using quotation marks to signal direct quotation

2. C

4. To repeat their words, "We have turned the corner."

6. C

8. "I could not believe the condition of my hometown," he wrote.

10. "Is the computer plugged in?" the technical support operator asked, prompting Harry to snarl, "Yes, I'm not a complete idiot."

EXERCISE 23.2 Using quotation marks for titles and definitions

2. My dictionary defines *isolation* as "the quality or state of being alone."

4. Kowinski uses the term *mallaise* to mean "physical and psychological disturbances caused by mall contact."

6. "The little that is known about gorillas certainly makes you want to know more," writes Alan Moorehead in his essay "A Most Forgiving Ape."

8. If you had ever had "Stairway to Heaven" running through your head for four days straight, you would not like Led Zeppelin either.

10. Amy Lowell challenges social conformity in her poem "Patterns."

EXERCISE 23.3 Using quotation marks appropriately

SUGGESTED ANSWERS

2. Television commercials have frequently used popular songs as an effective way to connect their product with good feelings in consumers' minds.

4. The strategy of using hit songs in commercials can backfire when the listeners don't like the song or like it too much to think of it as an advertising jingle.

6. The rights to many Beatles songs, such as "Revolution," are no longer controlled by the Beatles.

8. Many Iggy Pop fans wonder what on earth his song "Lust for Life" has to do with taking an expensive ocean cruise.

10. Do consumers love the songs of their youth so much that merely hearing a song in an ad will make them buy that car?

EXERCISE 24.1 Using parentheses and brackets

2. Are the media really elite, and are they really liberal, as talk-show regulars (Ann Coulter, for example) argue?

4. An article in the *Journal of Communication* discussing the outcome of recent U.S. elections explained that "claiming the media are liberally biased perhaps has become a core rhetorical strategy" used by conservatives (qtd. in Alterman 14).

6. However, liberals are not the only media watchdogs: right-wing organizations, including Accuracy in Media (AIM), also closely examine the way political stories are reported.

8. According to the site's home page, the purpose of Campaign Desk was "to straighten and deepen campaign coverage" as a resource for

voters (most of whom rely on media coverage to make decisions about the candidates).

10. And can we forget that as media consumers, we have an obligation to be an informed electorate (even though it's easy to pay attention only to the news that reinforces our own beliefs)?

EXERCISE 24.2 Using dashes

2. Nevertheless, extra charges seem to be added to more and more services all the time.

4. The hidden costs of service fees are irritating—people feel that their bank accounts are being nibbled to death.

6. The "convenience charges" that people have to pay when buying show tickets by telephone are often a substantial percentage of the cost of the ticket.

8. C

10. C

EXERCISE 24.3 Using colons

2. C

4. The sonnet's structure is effective in revealing the speaker's message: love has changed his life and ended his depression.

6. Even more important was what money represented: success, prestige, and power.

8. C

10. Reviewers agree that Halwani's book possesses these traits: readability, intelligence, and usefulness.

EXERCISE 24.5 Reviewing punctuation marks

SUGGESTED ANSWERS

2. Some parental efforts do help children; for instance, children whose parents read to them are more likely to enjoy books.

4. A new idea that is popular with many parents of young children is sign language.

6. By sixteen to eighteen months, most children are able to speak simple words and make themselves understood.

8. Garcia showed that parents could easily teach their children signs for words such as *please, more, sleepy,* and *hungry.*

10. Not surprisingly, parents bought the book (and then the video), and now sign-language classes for small children are easy to find.

12. C

14. The researchers who developed the study said that the best reason for parents to sign with their children was to allow the children "to communicate what they need and see."

16. Others contend that the children's hand movements stand for concepts, so the movements are sign language.

18. In fact, children who can use sign language are often especially eager to learn how to speak.

20. Any activity that gets parents to spend more time communicating with their children probably has its benefits.

EXERCISE 25.1 Capitalizing

2. The Battle of Lexington and Concord was fought in April 1775.

4. Accepting an award for his score for the film *The High and the Mighty,* Dmitri Tiomkin thanked Beethoven, Brahms, Wagner, and Strauss.

6. We drove east over the Hudson River on the Tappan Zee Bridge.

8. "Bloody Sunday" was a massacre of Catholic protesters in Derry, Northern Ireland, on January 30, 1972.

10. The town in the American South where I was raised had a statue of a Civil War soldier in the center of Main Street.

EXERCISE 26.1 Using abbreviations

2. The power tools, ordinarily used for sanding wood, are placed on a thirty-foot track and plugged in; the sander to reach the end first wins.

4. There are three divisions of belt sander races: the stock division, which races sanders right out of the box; the modified division, which allows any motor the owner wants to add; and the decorative division, which provides a creative outlet for sander owners.

6. The fastest sanders run on very coarse sandpaper—a number sixteen grit is an excellent choice if it's available.

8. The S-B Power Tool Co. in Chicago, maker of Bosch sanders, allows participants to race its tools, but the company does not underwrite races.

10. No one knows what percentage of the nation's power tools have been used for this kind of entertainment.

EXERCISE 26.2 Spelling out numbers and using figures

SUGGESTED ANSWERS

2. You could travel around the city for only sixty-five cents. (*Or* C)

4. C

6. C (*Or* 25 cents)

8. Three hundred seven miles long and eighty-two miles wide, the island offered little of interest.

10. The department received 1,633 calls and 43 letters.

EXERCISE 27.1 Using italics

2. Regional writers produced some American classics, such as Mark Twain's *Huckleberry Finn* and James Fenimore Cooper's *Last of the Mohicans.*

4. Some of the most prolific regional writers were women such as Kate Chopin, who wrote her first collection of short stories, *Bayou Folk*, to help support her family.

6. Chopin also departed from regional works to explore women's experiences of marriage, as in her short piece, "The Story of an Hour."

8. She later turned these into a novel, *Deephaven*, which she hoped would "teach the world that country people were not . . . ignorant."

10. Many regional stories—Stephen Crane's "The Bride Comes to Yellow Sky" is a prime example—show the writer's concern that an isolated culture is in danger of disappearing.

EXERCISE 28.1 Using hyphens in compounds and with prefixes

2. thirty-three

4. a politician who is fast-talking

6. a what-me-worry look

8. self-guided

10. C

EXERCISE 28.2 Using hyphens appropriately

2. The name of the president-elect had been announced an hour before the polls closed.

4. C

6. The ill-fated antelope became the baboon's lunch.

8. The badly wrapped sandwich oozed mustard and bits of soggy lettuce.

10. One of Baryshnikov's favorite dancers was Fred Astaire.

LANGUAGE

EXERCISE 30.1 Identifying stereotypes

2. *how few hours:* Overlooks all the other work academics do in addition to classroom teaching: grading, conferencing, committee work, research.

4. *everyone in France hates Americans:* Overlooks the fact that like people everywhere, people in France are individuals with widely varying points of view about Americans (and every other topic).

6. *Dropouts:* Assumes anyone who didn't finish high school chose not to finish and is therefore foolish, unmotivated, lazy, or (perhaps) a criminal.

8. *ambulance chasers:* Assumes that lawyers are frivolous and out to earn large fees in order to benefit from the pain of others.

EXERCISE 30.3 Rewriting to eliminate offensive references

SUGGESTED ANSWERS

2. All of the children in the kindergarten class will ask someone at home to help make cookies for the bake sale.

4. Acting as a spokesperson, Cynthia McDowell vowed that all elementary schoolteachers in the district would take their turns on the picket line until the school board agreed to resume negotiations.

6. Violinist Josh Mickle, last night's featured soloist, brought the crowd to its feet. (Or accept any version that omits mention of age and religion—both irrelevant here.)

8. Despite the plane's mechanical problems, the crew (or crew members) were able to calm the passengers and land safely.

10. Attorney Margaret Samuelson won her sixteenth case in a row last week.

EXERCISE 32.1 Using formal register

SUGGESTED ANSWERS

2. The young dancers stamped their feet so that their anklets jingled, and the audience watched them approvingly.

4. We decided not to buy a bigger car that got poor gas mileage and instead to keep our old Honda.

6. After she had raced to the post office at ten minutes to five, she realized that she had completely forgotten the fact that it was a federal holiday.

8. Moby Dick's enormous size was matched only by Ahab's obsessive desire to destroy him.

10. The class misbehaved so dreadfully in their regular teacher's absence that the substitute lost his temper.

EXERCISE 32.2 Determining levels of language

SUGGESTED ANSWERS

2. formal; *audience:* a prospective employer you want to impress

4. formal; *audience:* an informed audience whom you hope to convince

EXERCISE 32.3 Checking for correct denotation

2. apex; Correct word: nadir [or low point]

4. effected; Correct word: affected

6. C

8. delusion; Correct word: illusion

10. Retrofitting; Correct word: Reintroducing

EXERCISE 32.4 Revising sentences to change connotation

2. waltz away/little people who keep the company running/peanuts
   Rewrite: CEOs are highly compensated with salary, stock options, and pension funds while employees get comparatively little.

4. Tree-huggers/ranted
   Rewrite: Environmentalists protested the Explorer's gas mileage outside the Ford dealership.

6. Naive/stumble/blithely yank
   Rewrite: Voters not familiar with using a voting machine often will simply pull the handle without making informed choices.

8. mob/yelling/jabbing
   Rewrite: A large group of chanting, sign-waving protesters appeared.

EXERCISE 32.5 Considering connotation

SUGGESTED ANSWERS

A complete answer is provided for the first italicized word as a model.

2. *girl:* young lady, miss

4. *abide:* tolerate; *turns:* changes; *vital:* alive; *hold still:* contain their energy

EXERCISE 32.6 Using specific and concrete words

SUGGESTED ANSWERS

2. He has stained and crooked teeth, small eyes, and a few stray hairs that he considers a mustache on his upper lip, but he tells wonderful stories and has an enormous store of knowledge about subjects ranging from anthropology to political progressivism.

4. The Smollings' children rarely get invited to other peoples' homes because they squabble constantly, demand endless adult attention, break dishes, and jump on furniture.

6. Robert had a fever of 103 degrees and a rasping cough, so he stayed home from the holiday party at his office.

8. The feast at Mom's on Sunday was delicious as usual: roast chicken, garlic and sage stuffing, sweet garden peas, gallons of gravy, and half a fresh-baked apple pie each.

10. Few places in the United States display the wild climatic variations of central Texas: at one moment, the sky may be clear blue and the air balmy; at another, a racing flash flood may drown the landscape and threaten lives.

EXERCISE 32.7 Thinking about similes and metaphors

SUGGESTED ANSWERS

2. *great mounds of marshmallow fluff* (metaphor): clarifies the white and fluffy appearance of the clouds

4. *as if someone had punched him in the stomach* (simile): compares an emotion with a physical feeling

6. *like a magnolia corsage* (simile): makes vivid and concrete Mom Willie's heritage and suggests how positively she values it—and how proudly she "displays" it

8. *like water moving in a cavern* (simile): compares the sound of her voice to water in a cavern, helping the reader to imagine the sound

10. *lounging* (metaphor): compares the horse in pasture to people relaxing; *cuddling up* (metaphor): emphasizes the pleasure the writer has read-

ing mysteries; *top priority* (metaphor): reading as an activity of official importance

MULTILINGUAL WRITERS

EXERCISE 34.2 Using appropriate noun phrases

2. Dangerous germs such as salmonella are commonly found in some foods.

4. Many people regularly clean their kitchen counters and cutting boards to remove bacteria.

6. Every time someone wipes a counter with a dirty sponge, more germs are spread around the kitchen.

8. According to research studies, young single men's kitchens tend to have fewer germs than other kitchens.

EXERCISE 35.1 Identifying verbs and verb phrases

2. Holi <u>is known</u> as the festival of colors, not only because spring <u>brings</u> flowers, but also because Holi celebrations always <u>include</u> brightly colored dyes.

4. During Holi, people <u>toss</u> fistfuls of powdered dyes or dye-filled water balloons at each other and <u>sing</u> traditional Holi songs.

6. Any person who <u>is walking</u> outside during a Holi celebration <u>will</u> soon <u>be wearing</u> colored powders or colored water.

8. Many people <u>wear</u> white clothing for Holi.

10. <u>Doesn't</u> Holi <u>sound</u> like fun?

EXERCISE 35.3 Using specified forms of verbs

POSSIBLE ANSWERS

2. Someone followed the instructions too literally.
   Someone was following us as we drove to the beach.

4. The geese migrated to avoid a harsh winter.
   The geese are migrating late this year.

6. Those teenagers consumed three dozen hamburgers and two cases of pop.
   When I left the picnic, the teenagers were consuming the last of the carrot cake.

8.   The pasta steamed in the buffet tray.
     The pasta is steaming up the kitchen.

10. This hamburger tastes good.
     The hamburger had tasted fine until I noticed the fly on the bun.

EXERCISE 35.4 Identifying tenses and forms of verbs

2.   were talking: past progressive

4.   were arriving: past progressive; was getting: past progressive

6.   have attempted: present perfect

8.   has driven: present perfect

10. had forgotten: past perfect

EXERCISE 35.5 Using verbs appropriately

2.   The Rosetta Stone is *covered* with inscriptions in three ancient languages.

4.   At that time, scholars *had been* puzzled by hieroglyphics for centuries.

6.   A scholar named Jean François Champollion could *understand* both ancient Greek and modern Egyptian, known as Coptic.

8.   From the Demotic inscription, he *learned* to read the hieroglyphics.

10. The hieroglyphics and the Demotic and Greek texts all *contain* a decree from an ancient king.

EXERCISE 35.6 Using infinitives and gerunds appropriately

SUGGESTED ANSWERS

2.   Ashok refused to answer his sister's questions.

4.   C

6.   We appreciated getting the invitation.

EXERCISE 35.7 Writing conditional sentences

SUGGESTED ANSWERS

2.   If the dot-com boom had continued, that prediction might have come true.

4.   If any computer job is announced these days, hundreds of qualified people apply for it.

6. If Indian workers required as much money as Americans do to live, U.S. companies would not be as eager to outsource computer work to the other side of the world.

8. Would fewer Americans be unemployed right now if the dot-com boom had never happened?

10. If American students want to prepare for a secure future, they should consider a specialty such as nursing, in which jobs are available and the work cannot be sent abroad.

EXERCISE 36.1 Using prepositions idiomatically

2. in

4. in

6. on

8. with

10. to

EXERCISE 36.2 Recognizing and using two-word verbs

2. two-word verb

4. two-word verb

6. verb + preposition

8. two-word verb

10. two-word verb

EXERCISE 37.1 Expressing subjects and objects explicitly

SUGGESTED ANSWERS

2. C

4. There are problems with doing everything online, of course.

6. There are small-time thieves and pranksters disrupting online services.

8. A hacker can get enormous amounts of online data, even if the site is supposed to be secure.

10. Internet users must use caution and common sense online, but it is also essential for online information to be safeguarded by security experts.

EXERCISE 37.2 Editing for English word order

SUGGESTED ANSWERS

2. He displays a flag proudly in the window.

   OR

   He proudly displays a flag in the window.

4. She should not go into the woods alone.

6. Sandy drove extremely poorly during her first road test.

8. Some restaurant guests would like to begin with desserts.

10. "Speak English fluently," ordered the instructor.